FUNDAMENTALS OF FINANCIAL INSTITUTIONS AND MARKETS

ABEBE TILAHUN KASSAYE

Made with ❤ on the Notion Press Platform
www.notionpress.com

Fundamentals of Financial Institutions and Markets

By: - Abebe Tilahun Kassaye

Addis Ababa, Ethiopia

January, 2023

Table of Contents

Chapter One: - An overview of Financial System

Leaning Objectives

At the end of the chapter students/learners will be able to.

- *Identify the role of financial system in the economy*
- *Distinguish financial asset role and properties*
- *Recognize financial markets role, classifications and participants*
- *Acquaint with the concepts of lending and borrowing in the financial system*

1. Introduction

This chapter is designed to introduce you to the basic concepts of the Financial Systems. This chapter deals with the role of financial system in the economy, financial assets and its characteristics, financial markets role, classification and participants and finally discuss about lending and borrowing in the financial systems.

1. *The role of Financial System in the Economy*

Financial system performs the essential economic function of channelling funds from people who have saved surplus funds by spending less than their income to people who have a shortage of funds because they wish to spend more than their income.

Why is this channelling of funds from savers to spenders so important to the economy? The answer is that the people who save are frequently not the same people who have profitable investment opportunities available to them, the entrepreneur's. Let's first think about this on a personal level. Suppose that you have saved Birr 10,000 this year, but no borrowing or lending is possible because there are no financial systems. If you don't have an investment opportunity that will permit you to earn income with your savings, you will just hold on to the Birr 10,000 and will earn no interest. However, Germew the carpenter has a productive use for your Birr 10,000. He can use it to purchase a new tool that will shorten the time it takes him to build a house, there by earning an extra Birr 2000 per year. If you could get a touch with Germew, you could lend him t Birr 10,000 at an interest of 10% per year, and both of you would be better off. Because

In the absence of financial system, you and Geremew the carpenter might never get together. Without financial system, it is hard to transfer funds from a person who has no investment opportunities to one who has them; you would both be stuck with the status quo, and both of you would be worse off. Financial markets are thus essential to promoting economic efficiency.

The existence of financial systems is also beneficial even if someone borrow for a purpose other than increasing production in a business. Say that you are recently married, have a good job, and want to buy a house. You can earn a good salary, but because you have just started to work, you have not yet saved much. Over time you would have no problem saving enough to buy the house of your dreams, but by then, you would be too old to get full enjoyment from it. Without financial system, you are stuck; you can't buy the house and will continue to live in your tiny apartment.

If a financial system were set up so that people who had built up savings could lend you the money to buy the house, you would be more than happy to pay them some interest in order to own a home while you are still young enough to enjoy it. Then, you had saved up enough funds; you would pay back your loan. The overall outcome would be such that you would be better off, as would the persons who made you loan. They would now earn some interest, where as they would not if the financial system did not exist.

Financial systems have such an important function in allowing funds to move from people who lack productive investment opportunities to people who have such opportunities. By doing so, a financial system contributes to higher productive and efficiency in the overall economy. It also directly improve the well-being of consumers by allowing them to time their purchases better, they provide funds to young people to buy what they need and can eventually afford without forcing them to wait until they have saved up the entire purchase price. The Financial system that is operating efficiently improves the economic welfare of everyone in the society.

1. The Flow of Funds in the Financial System (Financial Transactions)

Financial systems are never static; they change constantly in response to shifting demands from the public, the development of technology and changes in laws and regulations. Competition in the financial market place forces financial institutions to respond to public need by developing new, better quality, and more convenient financial services.

Whether simple or complex, all financial systems perform at least one basic function. They move scarce funds from those who save and lend (surplus-budget units) to those who wish to borrow and invest (deficit-budget units). In the process, money is exchanged for financial assets however the transfer of funds from savers to borrowers can be accomplished in at least three different ways. These are: - *direct finance, semi-direct finance, and indirect finance.*

i. *Direct Finance*

Borrowers borrow funds directly from lenders in financial markets by selling them securities (also called financial instruments).Borrowers and lenders meet each other and exchange funds in return for financial assets. It is the simplest method of carrying financial transactions. You engage in direct finance when you borrow money from a friend and give him or her IOU (a promise to pay) or when you purchase stocks or bonds directly from the company issuing them. We usually call the claims arising from direct finance primary securities because they flow directly from the lender to the ultimate users of funds.

Flow of Funds

Figure 1.1; the flow of funds in the financial system (direct and indirect finance)

The principal lender- savers are households, but business enterprises and the government (particularly state and local government), as well as foreigners and their governments, sometimes also find themselves with excess funds and so lend them out. The most important borrower- spenders are business and the government (particularly the federal government) but households and foreigners also borrow to finance their purchases of cars, furniture, and houses.

- *The following can be visible draw backs of direct financing system:-*

i. Both borrower and lender must desire to exchange the same amount of funds at the same time.
ii. The lender must be willing to accept the borrower's IOUs (a promise to pay), which may be quite risky, illiquid or slow to mature.
iii. There must be a coincidence of wants between surplus and deficit – budget units in terms of the amount and form of a loan. Without that fundamentals coincidence, direct finance breaks down.
iv. Both lender and borrower must frequently incur substantial information costs simply to find each other.
v. The borrower may have to contact many lenders before finding the one surplus – budget unit with just the right amount of funds and willingness to take on the borrower's IOU.

i. *Semi direct Finance*

Early in the history of most financial systems, a new form of financial transaction appears which we call semi direct finance.

Borrower-Spenders (Deficit Budget Units)

Security brokers and dealers

Saver-Lenders

(Surplus Budget Units)

Primary

Securities

Proceeds of security sales (less fees and commission)

Primary

Securities

Flow of fund

Figure 1.2; the flow of funds in the financial system (semi-direct finance)

Here, some individuals and business firms become securities brokers and dealers whose essential function is to bring surplus and deficit budget units together – thereby reducing information costs.

- **Broker:** An individual or institution that provides information concerning possible purchases and sales of securities. Either a buyer or a seller of securities may contact a broker, whose job is simply to bring buyers and sellers together.
- **Dealer:** Also serves as a middle man between buyers and sellers, but the dealer actually acquires the seller's securities in the hope of marketing them at a more favourable price. Dealers take a position of risk because by purchasing securities outright for their own portfolios, they are subject to risk of loss if those securities decline in value.

iii. Indirect Finance/Financial Intermediation

The limitations of both direct and semi direct finance stimulated the development of indirect finance carried out with the help of financial intermediaries. The process of indirect finance using financial intermediaries (institutions), called financial intermediation, is the primary route for channelling funds from lenders to borrowers, (see figure 1.1 above)

Financial intermediaries issue securities of their own or buy securities issued by corporations and then sell those securities to investors.

Examples of such securities include: checking and saving accounts, health, life and accident insurance policies, retirement plan and shares in mutual fund.

1. They generally carry low risk of default
2. The majority can be acquired in small denominations
3. They are liquid (for most) and can be easily converted into cash with little risk of significant loss for the purchaser.

2. Financial Intermediaries /Institutions

The principal financial institutions /intermediaries fall in to three categories; depository institutions (banks), contractual and savings institutions, and investment institutions

i. Depository institutions (banks)

These are financial institutions that accept deposit from individuals and institutions and makes loans. They include commercial banks and **thrift** institutions (savings and loan associations, mutual savings banks, and credit unions.)

ii. Contractual savings institutions

These are financial institution such as insurance companies and pension funds, which acquire funds at periodic intervals on contractual basis

Since they can predict with reasonable accuracy how much they will have to pay out in benefits in the coming years, they don't have to worry as much as depository institutions about losing funds.

iii. Investment intermediaries

These are financial institutions which sale shares to individuals and use these funds to invest n a pool of assets. Example: mutual funds, investment banks, money market mutual funds etc.

3. Why are Financial Intermediaries and Indirect Finance so Important in Financial System?

As shown in figure 1.1. Funds also can move from lenders to borrowers by a second route called indirect finance because it involves a financial intermediary that stands between the lender-savers and the borrower-spenders and helps transfer funds from one to the other. A financial intermediary does this by borrowing funds from the lender-savers and then using these funds to make loans to borrower[1]spenders.

The process of indirect finance using financial intermediaries, called financial intermediation, is the primary route for moving funds from lenders to borrowers. Why are financial intermediaries and indirect finance so important in financial markets? To answer this question, we need to understand the role of **transaction costs**, **risk sharing**, and **information costs** in financial markets.

i. Transaction cost

The time and money spent in carrying out financial transactions are a major problem for people who have excess funds to lend. Financial intermediaries can substantially reduce transaction costs because they have developed expertise in lowering them and because their large size allows them to take advantage of **economies of scale**, the reduction in transaction costs per dollar of transactions as the size (scale) of transactions increases. For example, a bank knows how to find a good lawyer to produce an airtight loan contract, and this contract can be used over and over again in its loan transactions, thus lowering the legal cost per transaction. Because financial intermediaries are able to reduce transaction costs substantially, they make it possible for you to provide funds indirectly to people with productive investment opportunities.

In addition, a financial intermediary's low transaction costs mean that it can provide its customers with **liquidity services**, services that make it easier for customers to conduct transactions. For example, banks provide depositors with checking accounts that enable them to pay their bills easily. In addition, depositors can earn interest on checking and savings accounts and yet still convert them into goods and services whenever necessary.

ii. Risk Sharing

Another benefit made possible by the low transaction costs of financial institutions is that they can help reduce the exposure of investors to risk that is, uncertainty about the returns investors will earn on assets. Financial intermediaries do this through the process known as risk sharing They create and sell assets with risk characteristics that people are comfortable with, and the intermediaries then use the funds they acquire by selling these assets to purchase other assets that may have far more risk. Low transaction costs allow financial intermediaries to share risk at low cost, enabling them to earn a profit on the spread between the returns they earn on risky assets and the payments they make on the assets they have sold. This process of risk sharing is also sometimes referred to as **asset transformation** because, in a sense, risky assets are turned into safer assets for investors. Financial intermediaries also promote risk sharing by helping individuals to diversify and thereby lower the amount of risk to which they are exposed. **Diversification** entails investing in a collection (**portfolio**) of assets whose returns do not always move together; with the result that overall risk is lower than for individual assets. (Diversification is just another name for the old adage, *"don't put all your eggs in one basket."*) Low transaction costs allow financial intermediaries to do this by pooling a collection of assets into a new asset and then selling it to individuals.

iii. Asymmetric Information

If one party often doesn't know enough about the other party to make accurate decisions, we call there is asymmetric information. It creates two major problems; *adverse selection and moral hazard.*

a. *Adverse selection* ; this is the problem created by asymmetric information before the transaction occurs .Due to lack of information parties who are most likely to produce an undesirable (adverse) outcome may be selected , who are unlikely to pay back the loan .This leads to *credit risk* or **risk of default**.
b. *Moral hazard* ;this problem is created by asymmetric information after the transaction occurs .This means after taking the loan ,the borrower might engage in activities that are undesirable or immoral. This makes again the probability of the loan to be paid back less.

The problems created by adverse selection and moral hazard can be minimized by financial intermediaries. They can screen out good from bad credit risk thereby reduce losses due to adverse selection. They develop experts in monitoring and evaluating the parties they lend to, thus reduce risks associated with moral hazard.

- **Techniques to Solve the Problem of Adverse Selection**

a. *Private production and sale of information*

The solution to the adverse selection problem in financial market is to eliminate asymmetric information by furnishing people funds with details about the individuals or firms seeking to finance their investment activities .One way to get this material to saver- lender is to have private companies which collect and produce information, distinguishes good from bad credit risk and sell it to purchasers of securities. The problem in such tool is "*free rider problem* ", this occurs when people who don't have paid for takes advantage of information that other people have paid. This discourages the private production and sale of information.

b. *Government regulation*

Government could produce information to help investors distinguish good from bad firms and provides it to the public free of charge. This solution, however, would involve

In releasing negative information about firms, a practice might be politically difficult.

The second possibility to regulate financial markets is that government can enforce;

v. To adhere to standard accounting principle
v. To disclose information about their sales, assets, and earnings.

c. *Financial intermediaries*

Financial intermediaries such as banks become an expert on the production of information about firms so that it can sort out good credit risk from bad ones then it can acquire funds from depositors and lend to potential investors.

d. *Collateral and net worth*

Property promised to the lender if the borrower defaults reduces the consequences of adverse selection because it reduces the lenders losses in the event of loss. In case of default the lender can sell the collateral.

The firm's asset and liability can perform a similar role as collateral. If a firm has high net worth, even if it engages in investments that it to have negative [profit and defaults on its debt payments, the can take title to the firms net worth and sell it off. In addition, the more net worth a firm has, the less likely it is to default.

v. **Techniques Used to Solve the Problem of Moral Hazard**

The following are the major tools in solving the problems associated with moral hazard

a. *Production of information and monitoring*

The creditor can be engage in particular type of information production; monitoring the firm's activities , auditing the firm frequently and checking on what the firm is generally doing.

b. *Government regulations to increase information*

Government can also minimize moral hazard problems by forcing firms to adhere to standard accounting principles.. They also pass laws to impose criminal penalties on people who commit the immoral or undesirable acts.

c. *Net worth*

When the borrower's net worth is higher, the risk of moral hazard will be greatly reduced because the borrowers themselves have a lot to lose. The greater the borrowers net worth, the greater the borrowers incentive to behave in such away that the lender expects and desires

d. *Monitoring and enforcement of restrictive covenants*

A lender can insure that the borrower uses the money for the purpose intended by writing provisions (restrictive covenants) into the debt contract that restrict the firm's activities.

Restrictive covenants can encourage the borrowers to engage in desirable activities that makes the more likely to be paid back. It also requires a borrowing firm to provide information about its activity periodically in the form of reports.

e. *Financial intermediation*

As we have seen before the intermediaries making private loans receive the benefits of monitoring and enforcement will work to shrink the moral hazard problems in debt contracts. And the concept of moral hazard has provided us additional reason why financial intermediaries play a more important role in channelling funds from saver to borrower than marketable securities do.

2. *Role of Financial Assets and Its Properties*

Assets can be classified as tangible or intangible. A tangible e asset is one whose value depends on particular physical properties—examples are buildings, land, or machinery. Intangible assets, by contrast, represent legal claims to some future benefit. Their value bears no relation to the form, physical or otherwise, in which these claims are recorded.

Financial Assets are different from real or physical assets. Physical asset markets (also called "tangible" or "real" asset markets) are those for products such as wheat, coffee, real estate, computers, and machinery. Financial asset markets, on the other hand, deal with stocks, bonds, notes, mortgages, and other claims on real assets, as well as with derivative securities whose values are derived from changes in the prices of other assets. Buying share of any Bank/insurance is a "pure financial asset," while an option contract to buy this share after three/six month is an example for derivative security whose value depends on the price of shares in stock markets.

Therefore, the financial assets are the representations of real assets and they don't have physical usefulness. They only represent values of an underlying asset. Hence, essentially, stocks and bonds are pieces of papers that represent values and claims. They are commonly called financial instruments, like Common Shares; Preference Shares; Government Bonds; Corporate Bonds; etc. The financial assets can be grouped into two main categories such as debt instruments and equity instruments. The various debt instruments being used for financial transactions in financial market includes treasury bill, commercial papers, bonds, debentures , certificate deposit etc. and the equity instruments/claims includes shares preferred stock/share, common stock and convertible bond.

i. Role of Financial Asset

Financial assets have two principal economic functions. The **first** is to transfer funds from those who have *surplus funds to invest* to those who **need funds to invest** in tangible assets. The **second** economic function is to *transfer funds* in such a way as to *redistributetheunavoidable risk* associated with the cash flow generated by tangible assets among those seeking and those providing the funds. However, as we will see, the claims held by the final wealth holders are generally different from the liabilities issued by the final demanders' of funds because of the activity of financial intermediaries that seek to transform the final liabilities into the financial assets that the public prefers.

ii. Characterstics/Properties of Financial Asset

Financial assets have certain properties/characteristics which help to determine the intention of investors on financial assets being traded in financial market. Some of these are:

a. *Moneyness*-some of the financial assets are used as a medium of exchange to settle transactions and they termed /serve as money. This characteristic is a clearly desirable one for investors in the market.
b. *Divisibility and denomination*-divisibility relates to the minimum size in which a financial asset can be liquidated and exchanged for money. The smaller the size, the more the financial asset is divisible. Financial assets have varying degree of divisibility depending on their denomination.
c. *Reversibility*- is the cost of investing in financial securities and then getting out of it and back in to cash again. This property also called round trip cost. eg: deposits at bank
d. *Term to maturity*-is the length of the interval until the date when the instrument is scheduled to make its final payment, or the owner is entitled to demand liquidation.
e. *Liquidity*; it is the degree in which financial assets can easily be liquidated (sold) withouta loss in value. For this term most scholars argued that there is no uniformly accepted definition, but according to Professor James Tobin liquidity is defined in terms of "How much sellers stand to lose if they wish to sell immediately as against engaging in a costly and time-consuming search". Any financial asset which takes more time to convert in to cash is termed as illiquid asset. E.g.: Pension funds. Whereas the less the time taken to convert in to cash is a liquid one. e.g.: Deposits in banks.
f. *Convertibility*; is the ability of the financial assets to be convertible in to other financial assets. E.g. A corporate convertible bond is a bond that the bond holder can change in to equity shares.
g. *Currency*: Most financial assets are denominated in one currency, such as US dollar or Yen,

and investors must choose them with that feature in mind.

h. ***Cash flow and return predictability***: Are turn that an investor will realize by holding a financial asset depends on the cash flow that is expected to be received. This includes dividend payments on stocks and interest payments on debt instruments.

a. ***Complexity;*** some financial assets are complex in the sense that they are actually combinations of two or more simpler assets. To find the true value of such an asset, one must decompose it in to its component parts and price each component separately.

j. ***Tax status:-*** The returns on various financial assets are subject to tax status because they are taxable earnings. The tax authorities are interested in collection of taxes on earnings from financial assets as securities which are regarded as incomes for investors. However, the tax status on financial assets varies from one economy to another. The rate of such taxes on financial assets is also subject to variation from time to time depending on the interest of the government which must be adhered to by the tax authorities. The tax status on financial assets also differs from one type of security to another depending on the nature of the issuing companies or institutions such as Federal, State, or local government. For instance, tax on treasury bills is zero in Ethiopia while it is 10% on dividend from share companies.

3. *Roles of Financial Markets, Classifications and Participants*

Financial markets are places or circumstances that permit and facilitate the trade of financial assets. The stock exchanges, the bond markets are good examples of financial markets. It is a market in which funds are transferred or mobilized from people (transfer units) having an excess of available funds to those people (deficit) units with a shortage of funds to invest. As a market for financial claims, the main actors are households, business (including financial institutions), and government units that purchase/sell financial asset. In short those participants are broadly categorized in to surplus and deficit units. Financial markets provide quite a lot of benefits who come and transact assets. They will get funds if they need any provided they fulfil what is required of them. They offload excess funds on to profitable opportunities. Financial markets contribute a lot to the development of countries' economies. The various debt instruments being used for financial transactions in financial market includes treasury bill, commercial papers, bonds, debentures , certificate deposit etc. and the equity instruments/claims includes shares preferred stock/share, common stock and convertible bond.

i. Role of Financial Markets in Financial System

We have defined a financial market as a market for creation and exchange of financial assets. If you buy or sell financial assets, you will participate in financial markets in some way or the other. Financial markets play a pivotal role in allocating resources in an economy by performing three important functions:

a. Financial markets ***facilitate price discovery*** the continual interaction among numerous buyers and sellers who use financial markets helps in establishing the prices of financial assets. Well organized financial markets seem to be remarkably efficient in price discovery. That is why financial economists say" if you want to know what the value of a financial asset is, simply look at its price in the financial market".

b. Financial markets ***provide liquidity*** to financial assets. Investors can readily sell their financial assets through the mechanism of financial markets. In the absence of financial markets which provide such liquidity, the motivation of investors to hold financial assets will be considerably diminished. Thanks to transferability and negotiability of securities through the financial markets, it is possible for companies and other entities to raise long term funds from investors with short term and medium term horizons. While one investor is substituted by another when a security is transacted, the company is assured of long term availability of funds.

  c. Financial markets considerably **reduce transaction costs.** The two major costs associated with transacting are search costs and information costs. Search costs comprise of explicit costs such as the expenses incurred on advertising when one wants to buy or sell an asset and implicit costs such as the effort and time one has to put to locate a customer. Information costs refer to costs incurred in evaluating the investment merits of financial assets.

Besides, in line to the above functions the market can help participants to facilitate:

    v. the raising of capital/fund (in the capital market)
    v. international trade (currency /foreign exchange market)
    v. transfer of risks (in the derivative market)

ii. Classification of Financial Markets

Financial markets are classified under different bases to trade financial assets:

1. Based on Nature of Claim

a. *Equity market*-is the financial market for residual claims (equity instruments). Example stock market.
b. *Debt market*–the financial market for fixed claims (debt instruments). It is a market in which securities that require the issuer (the borrower) to pay the holder (the lender) certain fixed dollar amounts at regularly scheduled intervals until specified time (the maturity date) is reached, regardless of the success or failure of any investment projects for which the borrowed funds are used are going to be traded.

2. Based on Seasoning of Claim /issuance of financial asset

a. *Primary market*-is a market in which newly issued securities are traded.
b. *Secondary market*-is a market in which previously issued/second hand securities are traded. Also called after market

3. Based on maturity/term of claims

a. *Money market*-a market with shortly matured(less than a year) financial securities are being traded.
b. *Capital market*- a market with long period matured(greater than a year) financial securities are being traded.

4. Timing of Delivery

a. *Spot/cash market*: the market where the delivery occurs immediately the transaction occurs
b. *Derivative market;* is the market where the delivery occurs at a pre determined time in the future.

5. Based on organizational structure

a. *Organized exchange market (auction)*-is an organized and regulated financial market where securities are bought and sold at a price governed by demand and supply forces.

It is a market where buyers and sellers of securities (or their agents or brokers) meet in one central location to conduct trades. Example New York and American stock exchange

b. *Over the counter market (OTC)* –is a market made through brokers or dealers called market makers using a negotiation over telephone or computer based networking system.

iii. Participants of Financial Markets

Modern financial markets are characterized by the involvement of a variety of participants with a wide range of motivations. These include individuals, commercial and investment banks, financial institutions, investment companies, insurance and pension funds, businesses, multinationals, local and central government, and international institutions such as the European Investment Bank (EIB) and the World Bank, Treasuries and central banks. There are also brokers who act on behalf of a third party and regulators who seek to ensure the smooth functioning of market activity. The relative importance of the various market participants can vary greatly from one financial centre to another; over the years, however, there has been a pronounced increase in the relative importance of institutional investors, a process known as the institutionalization of financial markets. Institutional investors, because they buy and sell large volumes of securities, require a high degree of liquidity so that their trades do not adversely affect the share prices they deal in. **A broker** acts as an intermediary on behalf of investors wishing to conduct a trade; the broker is the legal agent of the investors. In return for executing a client's instructions, a broker obtains a commission for his services. Many brokers offer additional services such as investment advice, research, custody and other services. A market-maker acts as a dealer in a financial security, quoting both a price at which he is willing to buy a security (the bid price) and a higher price at which he is willing to sell the security (the ask price). The difference, or spread, between the bid-ask prices represents a profit margin. Market-makers provide liquidity for the market, a set of prices for investors and reliable price information. **Arbitrageurs, hedgers** and **speculators** in any financial market there are generally three different and important participants distinguished by their motivation for trading in the market.

Arbitrageurs Arbitrage has a very specific meaning within the context of financial markets; it is the process of exploiting price anomaly in order to make riskless guaranteed profits. Arbitrageurs are economic agents that buy and sell financial securities to make such profits. For example, if asset A trades at a higher price on market 1 than on market 2, then arbitrageurs will buy the asset in market 2 at the cheap price and immediately sell it in market 1 at the higher price. The very act of arbitrage has the effect of lowering the price of asset A in market 1 and raising the price in market 2, until the price differential and arbitrage opportunity is eliminated. The very fact that there is a risk[1]less guaranteed profit to be made means that arbitrage opportunities are relatively rare in today's financial markets. Even when they exist, they usually do so only for a very short space of time.

Hedgers Hedging is the process of buying or selling a financial asset in order to reduce or eliminate an existing risk. A hedger is a participant in financial markets who seeks to reduce or limit some risk by engaging in the purchase or sale of a financial security. Speculators Speculation is the process of taking on risk in the hope of making a profit.

A speculator is a participant in financial markets that assumes a risky or 'open' position in financial securities in the hope of making a profit. For example, if a speculator thinks security A is underpriced and likely to go up in price, he will purchase the security today and if the security goes up in price as he expects he will be rewarded with a profit. However, speculation is a risky business and security A may actually fall in price in which case the speculator will have to 'close' his position at a loss.

4. *Lending and Borrowing in the Financial System*

Finance means any activity that involves borrowing, lending, or sharing risks. Let's look at what happens in a financial market. In a financial market, we have borrowers meeting lenders. **Borrowers** are any agents who have investment opportunities, but who lack the cash to get those projects started. For instance, businesses might have an opportunity to make a profit if they could only borrow the money and build a factory. The government has the opportunity to build roads and bridges, but it is going to need to borrow the money to get those projects done. And finally, homeowners; that is, people who would like to buy a house and live in it, would be happy to do the transaction, but they are going to have to borrow money in the form of a mortgage before they can get their house off of the ground. So borrowers are people who have projects, ideas, but don't have cash on hand to pull them off.

Lenders on the other hand are people who have surplus cash and are looking for an opportunity to earn interest. They are looking for an opportunity to earn a rate of return on their money, but they don't have projects that they would like to do themselves. Therefore, getting lenders and borrowers together is an opportunity to make the economic pie bigger, and once these projects are underway, the borrowers can share their profits with the lenders. That is what happens in a financial market.

Let's look at the flow of funds in a financial market. What happens in this financial market is that lenders send cash to borrowers, so that they can purchase plant, equipment, houses, road crews, and things like that, to create the assets out of which profits are made. In return, the borrowers give the lenders an IOU. Now this term, IOU is not an acronym that stands for anything, it's a rebus, and it's a word picture, IOU money. And an IOU is a financial security, or a financial instrument. That is, it's a contract that explains what the lender is entitled to, at what date in the future, under what circumstances. That is, it tells the world and the lender what money to expect in the future as a result of this deal that the lender and the borrower have made. Now there are all different kinds of IOU's. There are bonds, which are debt contracts that entitle the lender to a fixed interest payment in the future. And, that is the way that most other loans work too, even if it is not a bond, the loan entitles you to a fixed interest payment if it is a debt instrument. There are also particular kinds of loans called treasury bills that are issued by the United States Government. These are short -term instruments that the government uses to finance its debt, and they entitle the lender to an interest payment within a year. There are also stock instruments, and stock or equity contracts entitle the lender to a share of the profits of this business venture at some date in the future (usually paid in the form of dividends).

Now, the borrower and the lender can get together directly, in which case they are engaging in a transaction we call direct finance. That is what would happen if you bought a share of IBM stock directly yourself, from a broker; or if you lent your sister money so that she could buy a car. That is direct finance, where the borrower and lender deal with one another directly, face to face; or through a broker. However, rather than going into the world of direct finance, you may want to reduce your search cost. That is, you may not want to spend time going out and looking for someone with a good project, plus there are risks involved, if you don't want to put all of your eggs in one basket. On top of that you are going to have to draw up a contract, and monitor compliance and all of that is going to involve a lot of transactions effort that you may want to spare yourself. Therefore, you are going to go through what is called a financial intermediary. And that is an agent in the economy that specializes in bringing lenders and borrowers together.

1. *Objectives*

At the end of the chapter students/learners will be able to.

- ◦ *Recognize financial institutions and capital transfer*
- ◦ *Appreciate the function of financial institutions*
- ◦ *Realize the roles of financial intermediaries*
- ◦ *Differentiate the classification of financial institutions*
- ◦ *Discriminate the types of risk in financial industry*

Text Box: Leaning Objectives At the end of the chapter students/learners will be able to. ü Recognize financial institutions and capital transfer ü Appreciate the function of financial institutions ü Realize the roles of financial intermediaries ü Differentiate the classification of financial institutions ü Discriminate the types of risk in financial industry

Chapter Two: - Financial Institutions in the Financial System

2.1. Financial Institutions and Capital Transfer

A *financial institution* is an organization that facilitates financial **transactions** and is a key player in financial intermediation. They are involved in handling transactions such as loans, deposits, and currency changes. The methods in which financial institutions work involve utilizing money from their clients and then allocate to people and organizations that need it.

Financial institutions include varying areas of business operations, including banks, investment dealers, and insurance companies. Business operations are integral in any economy as they handle different financial activities. Therefore, people and businesses rely on financial institutions to handle their transactions and investments at times. Due to their criticality, financial institutions need regulation mostly from a government since their insolvencies can lead to a national fright.

A *Funds Transfer* is a sequence of events that results in the movement of funds from the remitter to the beneficiary. It is also defined as the remittance of funds from one party to itself or to another party through the banking system. It is an essential support function for other financial products such as loan repayment, settlement of trade bills etc., apart from being an important stand-alone function in a typical bank.

Funds Transfers can be classified as Incoming, Outgoing or internal depending on the direction of flow of funds in the transfer. Incoming or Outgoing transfers are indicative of whether funds are coming in or going out of the bank. Internal transfers indicate funds being transferred within the bank itself (between two accounts within the Bank). No other financial institution is involved in such transfers. Based on the parties involved in the transfer, **Funds Transfers can also be classified** as customer transfer, bank transfer and bank transfer for own account.

- *Customer Transfer*: A customer transfer is a transfer in which either the ordering customer or the beneficiary customer, or both, are non-financial institutions, i.e. at least one party in the chain is not a financial institution.
- *Bank Transfer*: A bank transfer refers to the transfer of funds between the ordering institution and beneficiary institution. Here the originator and beneficiary and all intermediary parties are financial institutions.
- *Bank Transfer for Own Account*: A transfer initiated by a bank to transfer funds from one of its accounts (held in one Bank) to another account (held in another Bank)

2. *Functions of Financial Institutions*

There are multiple **functions of financial institutions**. They include:

a. *Banking services* - Financial institutions, specifically commercial banks, assist their customers by giving them banking services like deposit and saving services. These institutions also give out credit services that assist their clients in catering to their immediate needs. The credit services could include mortgages, personal or educational loans.
b. *Capital formation* - Financial institutions assist in the creation of capital by increasing capital stock. Financial institutions can increase the stocks by organizing savings that are not in current use by customers and giving them to investors.
c. *Monetary supply regulation* - Financial institutions control the supply of money in an economy. The main objective of this control is to ensure that there is stability in an economy and limited chances of inflation. The financial institution tasked with this responsibility is the central bank, and it completes this task by transacting the government's securities to influence liquidity.
d. *Pension fund services* - Pension funds are made by financial institutions to assist people in preparation for their retirement. These pension funds are investment means that these institutions create to ensure individuals have money after their retirement, which could be issued on a monthly basis.
e. *Ensure economic growth* of a nation - Governments play a vital role in controlling financial institutions, and the main objective is to help in the growth of an economy. When there are issues in an economy, financial institutions are mandated to provide loans with low interest to assist in maintaining an economy.

3. *Financial Intermediaries and their Roles*

Most people take for granted the ability of the financial system to shift resources from savers to investors, but when you look closely at the details, you're struck by how complicated the task is. It's amazing the enterprise works at all. Lending and borrowing involve both transactions costs, like the cost of writing a loan contract, and information costs, like the cost of figuring out whether a borrower is trustworthy. Financial institutions exist to reduce these costs.

a. **Pooling Savings:** - The most straightforward economic function of a financial intermediary is to pool the resources of many small savers. By accepting many small deposits, banks empower themselves to make large loans. To succeed in this endeavour pooling people's savings in order to make large loans the intermediary must attract substantial numbers of savers. This means convincing potential depositors of the institution's soundness. Banks are adept at making sure customers feel that their funds will be safe.

b. **Safekeeping, Payments System Access, and Accounting:** - We deposit our pay checks and entrust our savings to a bank or other financial institution because we believe it will keep our resources safe until we need them. When we think of banks, safekeeping is only one of several services that immediately come to mind. The others are Internet and mobile access, automated teller machines, credit and debit cards, checkbooks, and monthly bank statements. In providing depositors with these physical and electronic services, a bank gives them access to the payments system the network that transfers funds from the account of one person or business to the account of another. The bank provides depositors a way to get cash into their wallets and to finalize payments using credit cards, debit cards, and checks. And because banks specialize in handling payments transactions, they can offer all these services relatively cheaply. Financial intermediaries reduce the costs of financial transactions. Beyond safekeeping and access to the payments system, financial intermediaries provide bookkeeping and accounting services.

c. **Providing Liquidity and payment mechanism:** - One function that is related to access to the payments system is the provision of liquidity.

When a financial asset can be *transformed into money quickly*, easily, and at low cost, it is said to be very liquid. Financial intermediaries offer us the ability to transform assets into money at relatively low cost. That's what ATMs are all about converting deposit balances into money on demand. Most transactions made today are *not done with cash*. Instead, payments are made using checks, credit cards, debit cards, and electronic *transfers of funds*. These methods for making payments, called payment mechanisms, are provided by certain financial intermediaries. The liquidity services financial intermediaries provide go beyond fast and easy access to account balances. Intermediaries offer both individuals and businesses lines of credit, which are similar to overdraft protection for checking accounts. A line of credit is essentially a preapproved loan that can be drawn on whenever a customer needs funds.

d. **Diversifying Risk:** - Banks mitigate risk in a straightforward way: They take deposits from thousands or even millions of individuals and make thousands of loans with them. Thus, each depositor has a very small stake in each one of the loans. All financial intermediaries provide a low-cost way for individuals to diversify their investments. Mutual fund companies offer small investors a low-cost way to purchase a diversified portfolio of stocks and eliminate the idiosyncratic risk associated with any single investment.

e. **Collecting and Processing Information:** - One of the biggest problems individual savers face is figuring out which potential borrowers are trustworthy and which are not. Most of us do not have the time or skill to collect and process information on a wide array of potential borrowers. And we are understandably reluctant to invest in activities about which we have little reliable information. The fact that the borrower knows whether he or she is trustworthy, while the lender faces substantial costs to obtain the same information, results in an information asymmetry. Very simply, borrowers have information that lenders don't. By collecting and processing standardized information, financial intermediaries reduce the problems information asymmetries create. They screen loan applicants to guarantee that they are creditworthy. They monitor loan recipients to ensure that they use the funds as they have claimed they will.

A Summary of the Role of Financial Intermediaries

4. *Classifications of Financial Institutions*

Financial institutions are responsible for distributing financial resources in a planned way to the potential users. There are a number of institutions that collect and provide funds for the necessary sector or individual. Correspondingly, there are several institutions that act as the middleman and join the deficit and surplus units. Investing money on behalf of the client is another variety of functions of financial institutions. Basically, the services provided by the various types of financial institutions may vary from one institution to another

Broadly speaking financial institutions are categorized in to two major parts, as:

a. Depository financial institutions; which include *commercial banks, savings and loan associations, mutual savings banks*, and *credit unions*

b. Non-depository financial institutions; which comprises of *contractual savings institutions* (insurance companies and pension funds); *investment institutions* (finance companies, mutual funds, money market mutual funds, stock brokerage firms, investment banks etc)

At the same time, there are several governmental financial institutions assigned with regulatory and supervisory functions. These institutions have played a distinct role in fulfilling the financial and management needs of different industries, and have also shaped the national economic scene.

5. *Depository Financial Institutions*

Depository institutions are financial intermediaries that accept deposits from individuals and institutions and make loans. These institutions include commercial banks and the so-called **thrift institutions (thrifts)**: savings and loan associations, mutual savings banks, and credit unions. The primary functions of financial institutions of this nature are:

- Accepting Deposits;
- Providing Commercial Loans;
- Providing Real Estate Loans;
- Providing Mortgage Loans; and

○ Issuing Share Certificates.

Depository institutions are popular financial institutions for the following reasons:

- They offer deposit accounts
- They provide loan facilities
- They accept the risk on loans provided
- They have more expertise
- They diversify their loans among numerous deficit units

a. **Commercial Banks:**-The primary function of a commercial bank is to accept deposits. It is a for-profit financial institution that provides loans and other services to its clients. A commercial bank can be public or private, as well as domestic or foreign. The government will be a major stakeholder in public sector banks that operate under the supervision of the nation's central bank. Private sector banks are similar to limited liability companies in which shareholders are individuals and the banks are run as private businesses. Foreign banks will have many branches in various countries and will have their headquarters in another country. Commercial banks provide numerous services in our financial system. The services can be broadly classified as follows: (i) individual banking, (ii) institutional banking, and (iii) global banking. There are three sources of funds for banks: (i) deposits, (ii) non-deposit borrowing, and (iii) common stock and retained earnings. Banks are highly leveraged financial institutions, which mean that most of their funds come from borrowing there are several types of deposit accounts. Demand deposits (checking accounts) pay *no interest* and can be withdrawn upon demand. Savings deposits pay interest, typically below market interest rates, do not have a specific maturity, and usually can be withdrawn upon demand. Time deposits, also called certificates of deposit, have a fixed maturity date and pay either a fixed or floating interest rate.

b. **Saving and Loan Association:** - The basic motivation behind the creation of saving &Loans was the providing of funds for financing the purchase of a home. The collateral for the loans would be the home being financed. Saving & Loans are either mutually owned or have corporate stock ownership. "Mutually owned" means there is no stock outstanding, so technically the depositors are the owners. To increase the ability of S&Ls to expand the sources of funding available to bolster/strengthen their capital, legislation facilitated the conversion of mutually-owned companies in to a corporate stock ownership structure. To sum up, S&Ls offer deposit accounts to surplus units and channel these deposits to deficit units and unlike commercial banks, they concentrated *on residential mortgage loans* to the owners (shareholders) of the institutions.

c. **Saving banks:** - are institutions similar to, although much older than, S&Ls. they can be either mutually owned in which case they are called *mutual savings banks* or *stock holder owned*. Most savings banks are of the mutual form. While the total deposits at savings banks are less than S&Ls, savings banks are typically larger institutions. Asset structures of savings banks and S&Ls are similar. The principal source of funds for savings banks is deposits.

d. **Credit unions:** - are the smallest and the newest of the depository institutions. They are varying small co-operative lending institutions organized around a particular group and owned by their members, member deposits are called ***shares***. The distribution paid to members is therefore in the form of dividends, not interest. Examples of credit unions can be union members, employees of a particular firm. Credit unions are different from other depository institutions because they:

- Are non- profit

- Restrict their funds to provide loans to their members only

6. *Non-depository Institutions*

Non-depository financial institutions are intermediaries that cannot accept deposits but do pool the payments in the form of premiums or contributions of many people and either invest it or provide credit to others. Hence, non-depository institutions form an important part of the economy. These non-depository institutions are sometimes referred to as the **shadow banking system**, because they resemble banks as financial intermediaries, but they cannot legally accept deposits. Consequently, their regulation is less stringent, which allows some non-depository institutions, such as hedge funds, to take greater risks for a chance to earn higher returns. These institutions receive the public's money because they offer other services than just the payment of interest. They can spread the financial risk of individuals over a large group, or provide investment services for greater returns or for a future income.

The basic non-depository financial institutions include *insurance companies, pension funds, mutual funds, finance companies, investment banks* and *money market mutual funds* etc

a. **Insurance Companies:** - help to mobilize savings and investment in productive activities. In return, they assure investors against their life or some particular asset at the time of need. In other words, they transfer their customer's risk of loss to themselves.

- The primary function of insurance companies is to compensate individuals and corporations (policyholders) if perceived adverse event occur, in exchange for premium paid to the insurer by policyholder.
- Insurance companies provide (sell) insurance policies, which are legally binding contracts.
- Insurance companies promise to pay specified sum contingent on the occurrence of future events, such as death or an automobile accident.
- Insurance companies are risk bearers. They accept or underwrite the risk for an insurance premium paid by the policyholder or owner of the policy.

- Income of Insurance companies:

    ◦ Initial underwriting income (insurance premium)
    ◦ Investment income that occur over time

- Insurance companies can be classified in to *life insurance* and *general (Property-causality)* insurance
    - **Life insurance Companies**; Life insurance companies insure people against financial insecurities following a death and sell annuities (annual income payments upon retirement).They acquire funds from the premiums that people pay to keep their policies in force and use them mainly to buy corporate bonds and mortgages. Because claim payments are more predictable, life insurance companies invest mostly in long-term bonds, which pay a higher yield, and some stocks.
- **Property and Casualty Insurance;** These companies insure policyholders against loss from theft, fire, and accidents. They are very much like life insurance companies, receiving funds through premiums for their policies, but they have a greater possibility of loss of funds if major disasters occur. For this reason, they use their funds to buy more liquid assets than life insurance companies

b. **Pension funds** receive contributions from individuals and/or employers during their employment to provide a retirement income for the individuals. Most pension funds are provided by employers for employees. The employer may also pay part or all of the contribution, but an employee must work a minimum number of years to be vested—qualified to receive the benefits of the pension. Self-employed people can also set up a pension fund for themselves through individual retirement accounts or other types of programs. While an individual has many options to save for retirement, the main benefit of government-sanctioned pension plans is *tax savings*. Pension plans allow either contributions or withdrawals that are tax-free. As a consequence of the regular contributions and the tax savings, pension funds have enormous amounts of money to invest. And because their payments are predictable, pension funds invest in long-term bonds and stocks, with more emphasis on stocks for greater profits.

c. **Mutual Fund: -** A mutual fund (in US) or unit trust (in UK and India) raise funds from the public and invests the funds in a *variety* of financial assets, mostly equity, both domestic and overseas and also in liquid money and capital market. They are investment companies that pool money from investors at large and offer to sell and buy back its shares on a continuous basis and use the capital thus raised to invest in securities of different companies Mutual funds possess shares of several companies and receive dividends in lieu of them and the earnings are distributed among the shareholders on a pro rata basis. Mutual funds sell shares (units) to investors and redeem outstanding shares on demand at their fair market value. *Thus, they provide opportunity of small investors to invest in a diversified portfolio of financial securities. Mutual funds are also able to enjoy economies of scale by incurring lower transaction costs and commission.*

Advantage of Mutual Funds

i. Mobilizing small saving

- Direct participation in securities is not attractive to small investors because of some requirements which are difficult for them.
- MF mobilizes funds by selling their own shares, known as units. These funds are invested in shares of different institution, government securities, etc
- To an investor, a unit in a mutual fund means ownership of a proportionate share of securities in the portfolio of a mutual fund.

ii. Professional management

- Mutual funds employ professional experts who manage the investment portfolio efficiently and profitably.
- Investors are relieved of the emotional stress in buying and selling securities since MF take care of this function.
- The Professional managers act scientifically at the right time to buy and sell for their client, and automatic reinvestment of dividends and capital gains, etc

iii. Diversified investment/ reduced risks

- Funds mobilized from investors are invested in various industries spread across the country/globe.
- This is advantage to the small investors b/s they cannot afford to assess the profitability and viability of different investment opportunities
- MF provide small investors the access to a reduced investment risk resulting from diversification,

economies of scale in transaction cost and professional financial management

iv. Better liquidity

- There is always a ready market for the mutual fund units- it is possible for the investors to disinvest holdings any time during the year at the Net Asset Value (NAV)
- Securities held by the fund could be converted into cash at any time. Thus, mutual funds could not face problem of liquidity to satisfy the redemption demand of unit holders.

v. Investment protection

- Mutual funds are legally regulated by guidelines and legislative provisions of regulatory bodies (such as SEC in US, SEBI in India etc)

vi. Low transaction cost (economy of scale)

- The cost of purchase and sale of mutual funds is relatively lower because of the large volume of money being handled by MF in the capital market (economies of Scale)
  - Brokerage fees, trading commission, etc are lower
- This enhances the quantum of distributable income available for investors

vii. Economic Developments

- Mutual funds mobilize more savings and channel them to the more productive sectors of the economy
  - The efficient functioning of mutual funds contributes to an efficient financial system.
- This in turn paves ways for the efficient allocation of the financial resources of the country which in turn contributes to the economic development.

The investors' return in the mutual fund includes *capital appreciation* (capital gain from price appreciation of the underlying assets), and the *income generated* by the assets of the fund.

Mutual funds can be categorized in to two; open-*ended mutual funds and closed-ended mutual funds*

d. **Finance companies:** - raise funds by selling commercial paper (a short-term debt instrument) and by issuing stocks and bonds. They lend these funds to consumers, who make purchases of such items as furniture, automobiles, and home improvements, and to small businesses. Some finance companies are organized by a parent corporation to help sell its product. For example, Ford Motor Credit Company makes loans to consumers who purchase Ford automobiles.

e. **Investment bank:**- An investment bank is not the same as a commercial bank. The primary goal of investment bank is to advise business governments on how to meet their financial challenges. It helps their clients with financing, research, wealth management, asset management, IPO, provide advisory service on large project, mergers and acquisitions merger.

f. **Money Market Mutual Funds:** - These relatively new financial institutions have the characteristics of a mutual fund but also function to some extent as a depository institution because they offer deposit-type accounts. Like most mutual funds, they sell shares to acquire funds that are then used to buy money market instruments that are both safe and very liquid. The interest on these assets is then paid out to the shareholders.A key feature of these funds is that shareholders can write checks against the value of their shareholdings. In effect, shares in a money market mutual fund function like checking account deposits that pay interest.

7. *Risks in Financial Industry*

Risk has been defined in various ways across time. Some definitions focus on the probability of an event, others refer to the uncertainty of outcomes, positive or negative, and others to risks as the subset of uncertainty that can be quantified. Risk in finance is defined as the randomness of the return of investments, including both positive and negative outcomes. Under this view, a greater expected return is associated with a greater variability of outcomes.

In the financial industry, the view of risk is different. Risk is defined by the uncertainty that has adverse consequences on earnings or wealth, or the uncertainty associated with negative outcomes only. This view is that of regulators and risk managers. Regulations aim at enhancing the resiliency of financial firms and of the financial system in stressed conditions. Risk managers see their role as being accountable for identifying, assessing and controlling the likelihood and the consequences of adverse events for the firm. Under this view, risk is seen as the potential of loss resulting from the interaction with uncertainty. The interaction arises from the exposure of financial firms to such randomness. Exposure is the extent to which a business could be affected by certain factors that may have a negative impact on earnings.

Financial risks are defined according to the sources of uncertainty. The broad classes of financial risks are credit risk, market risk, liquidity risk and interest rate risk, divided into subclasses relative to the specific events that trigger losses.

a. **Credit risk**: - is the risk of losses due to borrowers' default or deterioration of credit standing. Default risk is the risk that borrowers fail to comply with their debt obligations. Default triggers a total or partial loss of the amount lent to the counterparty. Credit risk also refers to the deterioration of the credit standing of a borrower, which does not imply default, but involves a higher likelihood of default. The book value of a loan does not change when the credit quality of the borrower declines, but its economic value is lower because the likelihood of default increases. For a traded debt, an adverse migration triggers a decline of its quoted price. Recovery risk refers to the uncertain value of recoveries under default. Recoveries depend on the seniority of debt, on any guarantee attached to the transaction and on the workout efforts of the lender. The loss after workout efforts is the loss given default. Counterparty credit risk exists when both parties of a transaction are potentially exposed to a loss when the other party defaults. A swap contract exchanging fixed for floating interest flows between two parties is a typical example. The party who receives more than it pays is at risk with the other party. The exposure might shift from one party to the other, and its size varies, as a result of the movements of interest rates. Counterparty credit risk exists when exposures are market driven.

b. **Market risk**: - is the risk of losses due to adverse market movements depressing the values of the positions held by market players. The market parameters fluctuating randomly are called "risk factors": they include all interest rates, equity indexes or foreign exchange rates. Market risk depends on the period required to sell the assets as the magnitude of market movements tends to be wider over longer periods. The liquidation period is lower for instruments easily traded in active markets, and longer for exotic instruments that are traded on a bilateral basis (over the counter). Market risk is a price risk for traded instruments. Instruments that are not traded on organized markets are marked-to-market because their gains or losses are accounted for as variations of value whether or not materialized by a sale.

c. **Liquidity risk**: - is broadly defined as the risk of not being able to raise cash when needed. Banking firms raise cash by borrowing or by selling financial assets in the market. Funding liquidity refers to borrowing for raising cash. Funding liquidity risk materializes when borrowers are unable to borrow, or to do so at normal conditions. Asset liquidity refers to cash raised from the sale of assets in the market as an alternate source of funds, for example in market disruptions. Asset liquidity also refers to the risk that prices move against the buyer or seller as a result of its own trades when the market cannot absorb the transactions at the current price. Asset liquidity risk also arises when too many players do similar trades. For example, banks raising cash from liquidation of assets in the adverse conditions of the 2008 crisis faced substantial losses from the deep discounts in their trades. Extreme lack of liquidity results in failure. Such extreme conditions are often the outcome of other risks, such as major markets or credit losses. These unexpected losses raise doubts with respect to the credit standing of the organization, making lenders refrain from further lending to the troubled institution. Massive withdrawals of funds by the public, or the closing of credit lines by other institutions, are potential outcomes of such situations. To that extent, liquidity risk is often a consequence of other risks.

d. **The interest rate**: - risk is the risk of declines of net interest income, or interest revenues minus interest cost, due to the movements of interest rates. Most of the loans and receivables of the balance sheet of banks, and term or saving deposits, generate revenues and costs that are interest rate driven. Any party who lends or borrows is subject to interest rate risk. Borrowers and lenders at floating rates have interest costs or revenues indexed to short-term market rates. Fixed-rate loans and debts are also subject to interest rate risk. Fixed-rate lenders could lend at higher than their fixed rate if rates increase and fixed-rate borrowers could benefit from lower interest rates when rates decline. Both are exposed to interest rate fluctuations because of their opportunity costs arising from market movements.

e. **Foreign exchange risk**: - is the risk of incurring losses due to fluctuations of exchange rates. The variations of earnings result from the indexation of revenues and charges to exchange rates or from the changes of the values of assets and liabilities denominated in foreign currencies (translation risk).

f. **Solvency risk**: - is the risk of being unable to absorb losses with the available capital. According to the principle of "capital adequacy" promoted by regulators, a minimum capital base is required to absorb unexpected losses potentially arising from the current risks of the firm. Solvency issues arise when the unexpected losses exceed the capital level, as it did during the 2008 financial crisis for several firms. This capital buffer sets the default probability of the bank, the probability that potential losses exceed the capital base.

g. **Operational risks**: - are those of malfunctions of the information system, of reporting systems, of internal risk monitoring rules and of procedures designed to take corrective actions on a timely basis. The regulators define operational risk as "the risk of direct or indirect loss resulting from inadequate or failed internal processes, people and systems or from external events". The focus on operational risk developed when regulators imposed that the operational risks should be assigned a capital charge.

Risk-taking is an inherent element of banking and, indeed, profits are in part the reward for successful risk taking. In contrary, excessive, poorly managed risk can lead to distresses and failures of banks. Risks are, therefore, warranted when they are understandable, measurable, controllable and within a bank's capacity to withstand adverse results.

1. *Objectives*

At the end of the chapter students/learners will be able to.

Text Box: Leaning Objectives At the end of the chapter students/learners will be able to. ü Understand the theory and Structure of Interest Rates ü Recognize Factors Affecting Structure of Interest Rate Determinations   Chapter

Three: - Interest Rates in the Financial System

1. *The theory and Structure of Interest Rates*

Interest rates are among the most closely watched variables in the economy. Their movements are reported almost daily by the news media, because they directly affect our everyday lives and have important consequences for the health of the economy. They affect personal decisions such as whether to consume or save, whether to buy a house, and whether to purchase bonds or put funds into a savings account. Interest rates also affect the economic decisions of businesses and households, such as whether to use their funds to invest in new equipment for factories or to save their money in a bank.

3.1.1. Theory of Interest Rate

An interest rate is the price paid by a borrower (or debtor) to a lender (or creditor) for the use of resources during some interval. The amount of the loan is the principal, and the price paid is typically expressed as a percentage of the principal per unit of time (generally, a year). In this section, we present the two most influential theories of the determination of the interest rate: *Fishers theory of interest, which underlies the loanable funds theory*, and *Keynes's liquidity preference theory of interest*.

i. The Loanable Fund Theory: -

Irving Fisher analyzed the determination of the level of the interest rate in an economy by inquiring why people save (that is, why they do not consume all their resources) and why others borrow economy contains only individuals who consume and save with their current income, firms that borrow unconsumed income in loans and invest, a market where savers make loans of resources to borrowers, and projects in which firms invest. The interest rate on loans embodies no premium for default risk because borrowing firms are assumed to meet all obligations. Saving is the *choice between current* and *future consumption* of goods and services. Individuals save some of their current income in order to be able to consume more in the future. A chief influence on the saving decision is the individual's marginal rate of *time preference*, which is the willingness to trade some consumption now for more future consumption. Individuals differ in their time preferences. Some people may have a rate of *time preference* that leads them to forgo current consumption for an increase of 10% in their future consumption, while others might save only if their future consumption possibilities rise by 20%. Another influence on the saving decision is *income.* Generally, higher current income means the person *will save more*, although people with the same income may have different time preferences. The *third* variable affecting savings is the *reward for saving*, or the rate of interest on loans that savers make with their unconsumed income. Interest is what borrowers pay for the loans, and it makes greater future consumption possible. As the *interest rate rises*, each person becomes *willing to save more*, given that person's rate of time preference.

This description of the savings decision applies to all the people in the economy. The total savings (or the total *supply of loans*) available at any time is the sum of everybody's savings and a *positive function of the interest rate*. The relationship between *total savings* and the interest rate is graphed as the upward sloping supply function which relates the amount of savings/investment on the horizontal axis to the interest rate on the vertical axis.

The maximum that a firm will invest depends on the rate of interest, which is the cost of loans. The firm will invest only as long as the **marginal productivity of capital exceeds** or equals the **rate of interest**. In other words, firms will accept only projects whose **gain is not less than their cost of financing**. Thus, the firm's demand for borrowing is negatively related to the interest rate. If the rate is high, only limited borrowing and investment make sense. At a low rate, *more projects offer a profit*, and the firm wants to borrow more. This negative relationship exists for each and all firms in the economy. The economy's total demand for borrowed resources (or loans of unconsumed income), as a function of the interest rate, appears as the downward-sloping line labeled D.

The equilibrium rate of interest is determined by the interaction of the supply and demand functions. As a cost of borrowing and a reward for lending, the rate must reach the point where total supply of savings equals total demand for borrowing and investment. Figure 2-1 shows that this equilibrium rate of interest, labeled i, occurs at the intersection of the demand and supply curves, D and S. The equilibrium level of savings (which is the same as the equilibrium level of borrowing and investment) is given as SI. Clearly, Fisher's theory emphasizes that the long-run level of the *interest rate* and the amount of *investment depend* on a *society's propensity to save* and on *technological development*.

ii. *Liquidity preference:-*

It was proposed by J. M. Keynes back in 1936 which explain how interest rates are determined based on the preferences of households to hold money balances rather than spending or investing those funds. Saving and investment of market participants under economic uncertainty may be much more influenced *by expectations* and by *exogenous shocks* than by *underlying real forces*. A possible response of risk-averse savers is to vary the form in which they hold their financial wealth depending on their expectations about asset prices. Since they are concerned about the risk of loss in the value of assets, they are likely to vary the average liquidity of their portfolios. Liquidity preference is preference for holding financial wealth in the form of short-term, highly liquid assets rather than long-term illiquid assets, based principally on the fear that long-term assets will lose capital value over time. Money balances can be held in the form of currency or checking accounts, however it does earn a very low interest rate or no interest at all. A key element in the theory is the motivation for individuals to hold money balance despite the loss of interest income. Money is the most liquid of all financial assets and, of course, can easily be utilized to consume or to invest. The quantity of money held by individuals depends on their level of income and, consequently, for an economy the demand for money is directly related to an economy's income. There is a trade-off between holding money balance for purposes of maintaining liquidity and investing or lending funds in less liquid debt instruments in order to earn a competitive market interest rate. The difference in the interest rate that can be earned by investing in interest-bearing debt instruments and money balances represents an opportunity cost for maintaining liquidity. The lower the opportunity cost, the greater the demand for money balances; the higher the *opportunity cost*, the lower the demand for money balance.

3.1.2. Structures of Interest Rate

i. Risk Structure of Interest Rates

The risk structure of interest rates (the relationship among interest rates on bonds with same maturities) is explained by three factors: ***default risk, liquidity, and income tax consideration***

a. Default Risk:

One attribute of a bond that influences its interest rate is its default risk which occurs when the issuer of the bond is unable or unwilling to make interest payments when promised or pay off its face value when the bond matures. As the bonds default risk increases, the risk premium on that bond (the difference between *its interest rate* and the *interest rate on a default free treasury bond*) rises.

b. Liquidity:

Another attribute of a bond that influences its interest rate is its liquidity. A liquid asset is one that can be quickly and cheaply converted in to cash if the need arises. The more liquid an asset is the more desirable it is. Government treasury bonds are the most liquid of all long term bonds because they are so widely traded that they are the easiest to sell and the cost of selling them is low. Corporate bonds are *not* as such liquid because fewer for any one corporation are traded; thus it can be costly to sell these bonds in an emergency because it may be hard to find buyers quickly.

c. Income tax consideration:

Investors are more concerned with ***after-tax income*** than ***before-tax income*** earned on securities. If all other characteristics are similar, taxable securities must offer a higher before-tax yield than tax-exempt securities. The extra compensation required on taxable securities depends on the tax rates of individual and institutional investors. Investors in high *tax brackets benefit* most from tax-exempt securities. When assessing the expected yields of various securities with similar risk and maturity, it is common to convert them into an after-tax form, as follows:-

Illustrative example: - Consider a taxable security that offers a before-tax yield of 8 percent. When converted into after[1]tax terms, the yield will be reduced by the tax percentage. The precise after-tax yield is dependent on the tax rate T. If the tax rate of the investor is 20 percent, then the after-tax yield will be.....

Given Required **Solution**

$Y_{bt} = 8\%$ after tax rate $Y_{at} = Y_{bt}(1 - T) = Yat = 0.08(1\text{-}02) = 0.08(0.8) = \underline{\mathbf{0.064}} = \underline{\mathbf{6.4\%}}$

$T = 20\%$

ii. Term to Maturity Structure of Interest Rates

We have seen how risk, liquidity, and tax considerations (collectively embedded in the risk structure of interest rates) can influence interest rates. Another factor that influences the interest rate on a bond is its *term to maturity.* Bonds with identical risk, liquidity and tax characteristics may have different interest rates because *the time remaining to maturity is different*. The relationship between the yields on comparable securities but different maturities is called the **term structure of interest rates**. The primary focus here is the Treasury market. The graph which depicts the relationships between the interest rates payable on bonds with different lengths of time to maturity is called *the yield curve*. That is, it shows the term structure of interest rates.

The focus on the Treasury yield curve functions is due mainly because of its role as a benchmark for setting yields in many other sectors of the debt market. However, a Treasury yield curve based on observed yields on the Treasury market is an unsatisfactory measure of the relation between *required yield* and *maturity*. The key reason is that securities with the *same maturity* may actually provide *different yields*. Hence, it is necessary to develop more accurate and reliable estimates of the Treasury yield curve. It is important to estimate the theoretical interest rate that the Treasury would have to pay assuming that the security it issued is a zero-coupon security. If the term structure is plotted at a given point in time, based on the yield to maturity, or the spot rate, at successive maturities against maturity, one of the three shapes of the yield curve would be observed.

The type of yield curve, when the *yield increases* with maturity, is referred to as an *upward-sloping yield curve* or a *positively sloped yield curve*.

A distinction is made for upward sloping yield curves based on the steepness of the yield curve. The steepness of the yield curve is typically measured in terms of the maturity spread between the long-term and short-term yields.

A *downward-sloping* or *inverted yield curve* is the one, where yields in general *decline* as maturity increases.

A variant of the *flat yield* is the one in which the yield on short-term and long-term Treasuries are similar. But the yield on intermediate-term Treasuries are much lower than, for example, the six-month and 30-year yields. Such a yield curve is referred to as a *humped yield curve*.

YTM A: Upward slopping YTM B: Downward slopping

Description: Flat Yield   Description: Humped Yield
Curve   Curve

YTM C: Flat YTM D: Humped

iii. Theories of term structure of interest rates

There are several major economic theories that explain the observed shapes of the yield curve:

- *Expectations theory*
- *Liquidity premium theory*
- *Market segmentation theory*

a. Expectations theory

The pure expectations theory assumes that investors are indifferent between investing for a long period on the one hand and investing for a shorter period with a view to reinvesting the principal plus interest on the other hand. For example an investor would have no preference between making a 12-month deposit and making a 6-month deposit with a view to reinvesting the proceeds for a further six months so long as the expected interest receipts are the same. This is equivalent to saying that the pure expectations theory assumes that investors treat alternative maturities as perfect substitutes for one another. The pure expectations theory assumes that investors are risk-neutral. A risk-neutral investor is not concerned about the possibility that interest rate expectations will prove to be incorrect, so long as potential favourable deviations from expectations are as likely as unfavourable ones. Risk is not regarded negatively.

However, most investors are risk-averse, i.e. they are prepared to forgo some investment return in order to achieve greater certainty about return and value of their investments. As a result of risk-aversion, investors may not be indifferent between *alternative maturities*. Attitudes to risk may generate preferences for either short or long maturities. If such is the case, the term structure of interest rates (the yield curve) would reflect risk premiums. If an investment is close to maturity, there is little risk of capital loss arising from interest rate changes. A bond with a distant maturity (long duration) would suffer considerable capital loss in the event of a large rise in interest rates. The risk of such losses is known as **capital risk**. To compensate for the risk that capital loss might be realized on long-term investments, investors may require a risk premium on such investments. A risk premium is an addition to the interest or yield to compensate investors for accepting risk. This results in an upward slope to a yield curve. This tendency towards an upward slope is likely to be reinforced by the preference of many borrowers to borrow for long periods (rather than borrowing for a succession of short periods).

Some investors may prefer long maturity investments because they provide greater certainty of income flows. This uncertainty is **income risk**. If investors have a preference for predictability of interest receipts, they may require a higher rate of interest on short term investments to compensate for income risk. This would tend to cause the yield curve to be inverted (downward sloping). The effects on the slope of the yield curve from factors such as capital risk and income risk are in addition to the effect of expectations of future short-term interest rates. If money market participants expect short-term interest rates to rise, the yield curve would tend to be upward sloping. If the effect of capital risk were greater than the effect of income risk, the upward slope would be steeper. If market expectations were that short-term interest rates would fall in the future, the yield curve would tend to be downward sloping. A dominance of capital-risk aversion over income-risk aversion would render the downward slope less steep (or possibly turn a downward slope into an upward slope).

b. **Liquidity premium theory**

Some investors may prefer to *own shorter rather* than *longer term securities* because a shorter maturity represents greater liquidity. In such case they will be willing to hold long term securities only if compensated with a premium for the lower degree of liquidity. Though long-term securities may be liquidated prior to maturity, their prices are more sensitive to interest rate movements. Short-term securities are usually considered to be more liquid because they are more likely to be converted to cash without a loss in value. Thus there is a liquidity premium for less liquid securities which changes over time. The impact of liquidity premium on interest rates is explained by liquidity premium theory.

c. **Market segmentation theory**

According to the market segmentation theory, interest rates for different maturities are determined independently of one another. The interest rate for short maturities is determined by the supply of and demand for short-term funds. Long-term interest rates are those that equate the sums that investors wish to lend long term with the amounts that borrowers are seeking on a long-term basis. According to market segmentation theory, investors and borrowers do not consider their short-term investments or borrowings as substitutes for long-term ones. This lack of substitutability keeps interest rates of differing maturities independent of one another.

If investors or borrowers considered alternative maturities as substitutes, they may switch between maturities. However, if investors and borrowers switch between maturities in response to interest rate changes, interest rates for different maturities would no longer be independent of each other. An interest rate change for one maturity would affect demand and supply, and hence interest rates, for other maturities.

3.1.3. Measuring Interest Rates

Different debt instruments have very different streams of payment with very different timing. Thus we first need to understand how we can compare the value of one kind of debt instrument with another before we see how interest rates are measured. To do this, we make use of the concept of *present value*. The concept of **present value** (or **present discounted value**) is based on the commonsense notion that a birr paid to you one year from now is less valuable to you than a birr paid to you today: This notion is true because you can deposit a birr in a savings account that earns interest and have more than a birr in one year.

Let's look at the simplest kind of debt instrument, which we will call a **simple loan**. In this loan, the lender provides the borrower with an amount of funds (called the *principal*) that must be repaid to the lender at the *maturity date*, along with an additional payment for the interest. For example, if you made your friend, a simple loan of $100 for one year, you would require him/her to repay the principal of $100 in one year's time along with an additional payment for interest; say, $10. In the case of a simple loan like this one, the interest payment divided by the amount of the loan is a natural and sensible way to measure the interest rate. This measure of the so called *simple interest rate*, i, is:

If you make this $100 loan for one year, two years, three years or for *n* years, you would have

The process of calculating the future value of dollars received today, as we have seen above, is called *compounding the present*

The process of calculating today's value of dollars received in the future is called *discounting the future*. We can generalize this process by writing today's (present) value of $100 as *PV*, the future value of $133 as *FV*, and replacing 0.10 (the 10% interest rate) by *i*. This leads to the following formula:

In terms of the timing of their payments, there are four basic types of credit market instruments.

1. *A simple loan,* which we have already discussed, in which the lender provides the borrower with an amount of funds, which must be repaid to the lender at the maturity date along with an additional payment for the interest. Many money market instruments are of this type: for example, commercial loans to businesses.

2. A **fixed-payment loan:** (which is also called a **fully amortized loan**) in which the lender provides the borrower with an amount of funds, which must be repaid by making the same payment every period (such as a month), consisting of part of the principal and interest for a set number of years. For example, if you borrowed $1,000, a fixed-payment loan might require you to pay $126 every year for 25 years. Installment loans (such as auto loans) and mortgages are frequently of the fixed-payment type.

3. A **coupon bond** pays the owner of the bond a fixed interest payment (coupon payment) every year until the maturity date, when a specified final amount (**face value** or **par value**) is repaid. The coupon payment is so named because the bondholder used to obtain payment by clipping a coupon off the bond and sending it to the bond issuer, who then sent the payment to the holder. Nowadays, it is no longer necessary to send in coupons to receive these payments. A coupon bond with $1,000 face value, for example, might pay you a coupon payment of $100 per year for ten years, and at the maturity date repays you the face value amount of $1,000. (The face value of a bond is usually in $1,000 increments.)

A coupon bond is identified by three pieces of information. *First* is the corporation or government agency that *issues* the bond. *Second* is the maturity date of the bond. *Third* is the bond's **coupon rate**, the dollar amount of the yearly coupon payment expressed as a percentage of the face value of the bond. In our example, the coupon bond has a yearly coupon payment of $100 and a face value of $1,000. The coupon rate is then $100/$1,000 = 0.10, or 10%.

Capital market instruments such as Government Treasury bonds and notes and corporate bonds are examples of coupon bonds.

4. A **discount bond** (also called a **zero-coupon bond**) is bought at a price below its face value (at a discount), and the face value is repaid at the maturity date. Unlike a coupon bond, a discount bond does not make any interest payments; it just pays off the face value. For example, a discount bond with a face value of $1,000 might be bought for $900; in a year's time the owner would be repaid the face value of $1,000.Treasury bills and long-term zero-coupon bonds are examples of discount bonds.

These four types of instruments require payments at different times: *Simple loans* and *discount bonds make payment only at their maturity dates*, whereas *fixed-payment loans and coupon bonds have payments periodically until maturity.* How would you decide which of these instruments provides you with more income? They all seem so different because they make payments at different times. To solve this problem, we use the concept of present value, explained earlier, to provide us with a procedure for measuring interest rates on these different types of instruments.

Now, let us look at how the yield to maturity/interest rate is calculated for the four types of credit market instruments.

Simple Loan: Using the concept of present value, the yield to maturity on a simple loan is easy to calculate. For the one-year loan we discussed, today's value is $100, and the payments in one year's time would be $110 (the repayment of $100 plus the interest payment of $10). We can use this information to solve for the yield to maturity i by recognizing that the present value of the future payments must equal today's value of a loan. Making today's value of the loan ($100) equal to the present value of the $110 payment in a year gives us:

Solving for i

This calculation of the yield to maturity should look familiar, because it equals the interest payment of $10 divided by the loan amount of $100; that is, the yield to maturity equals the simple interest rate on the loan.

Fixed-Payment Loan: Recall that this type of loan has the same payment every period throughout the life of the loan. On a fixed-rate mortgage, for example, the borrower makes the same payment to the bank every month until the maturity date, when the loan will be completely paid off. To calculate the yield to maturity for a fixed-payment loan, we follow the same strategy we used for the simple loan—we equate today's value of the loan with its present value. Because the fixed-payment loan involves more than one payment, the present value of the fixed-payment loan is calculated as the sum of the present values of all payments

Example; Consider a loan of $1000 with fixed annual payments of $126 for the next 25 years.

Making today's value of the loan ($1,000) equal to the sum of the present values of all the yearly payments gives us:

For a fixed payment loan amount, the fixed yearly payment and the number of years until maturity are known quantities, and only the yield to maturity is not. So, solve for i.

Coupon Bond- To calculate the yield to maturity for a coupon bond, follow the same strategy for the fixed payment loan; equate today's value of the bond with its present value.

It is calculated as the sum of the present values of all the coupon payments plus the present value of the final payment of the face value of the bond.

= Price of coupon bond

C = yearly coupon payment

FV = Face value of the bond

n= Years to maturity date

General formula:

Example: What is the price of a 10% coupon bond with a face value of $1000, a 10% yield to maturity, and eight years to maturity?

Solution: Annual coupon (C) = 10%   1000 = 100

Three interesting facts:

1. When the coupon bond is priced at its face value, the yield to maturity equals the coupon rate. In other words, when the coupon rate is equal to the yield to maturity, the price of the bond will be equal to its par value

2. If the *yield to maturity* is greater than the *coupon rate*, the bond will be priced below its face value. A bond selling below par value is termed as *a discount bond.* For instance if the market interest rate in the above example rises to 12.25%, the bond will sell for $889.20.

3. If the yield to maturity is less than the coupon rate, the bond is priced above its par value; hence a bond selling above par value is called as a *premium bond.* Assume the market interest rate falls to 6% in the above example, the price of the bond will be $1249.40

Generally, the price of a coupon bond and the yield to maturity are negatively related; that is, as the *yield to maturity rises*, the *price of the bond falls*. If the *yield to maturity falls*, the price of the bond rises.

To explain why the bond price declines when the interest rate rises is that a higher interest rate implies that the future coupon payments and final payment are worthless when discounted back to the present; hence the price of the bond must be lower.

Discount Bond: the yield to maturity calculation for a discount bond is similar to that of the simple loan.

Example: If a $ 1000 face value, 1 year maturity bond is currently selling at $ 900, what will be its yield to maturity?

Where; FV = Face Value of the bond and   = current price of the discount bond

4. Real versus Nominal Interest Rates

So far in our discussion of interest rates, we have ignored the effects of inflation on the cost of borrowing. What we have up to now been calling the interest rate makes no allowance for inflation, and it is more precisely referred to as the **nominal interest rate**, which is distinguished from the **real interest rate**, the interest rate that is adjusted by subtracting expected changes in the price level (inflation) so that it more accurately reflects the true cost of borrowing. The real interest rate is more accurately defined by the *Fisher equation*, named for Irving Fisher, one of the great monetary economists of the twentieth century.

The Fisher equation states that the nominal interest rate *i* equals the real interest rate   plus the expected

rate of inflation

Rearranging terms, we find that the real interest rate equals the nominal interest rate minus the expected inflation rate:

To see why this definition makes sense, let us first consider a situation in which you have made a one-year simple loan with a 5% interest rate ($i = 5\%$) and you expect the price level to rise by 3% over the course of the

year (   ). As a result of making the loan, at the end of the year you will have 2% more in **real terms**, that is, in terms of real goods and services you can buy. In this case, the interest rate you have earned in terms of real goods and services is 2%; that is,

Now what if the interest rate rises to 8%, but you expect the inflation rate to be 10% over the course of the year? Although you will have 8% more dollars at the end of the year, you will be paying 10% more for goods; the result is that you will be able to buy 2% fewer goods at the end of the year and you are 2% worse off *in real terms*. This is also exactly what the Fisher definition tells us, because:

As a lender, you are clearly less eager to make a loan in this case, because in terms of real goods and services you have actually earned a negative interest rate of 2%. By contrast, as the borrower, you fare quite well because at the end of the year, the amounts you will have to pay back will be worth 2% less in terms of goods and services—you as the borrower will be ahead by 2% in real terms. ***When the real interest rate is low, there are greater incentives to borrow and fewer incentives to lend.***

2. *Factors Affecting Structure of Interest Rate Determinations*

Although it is useful to identify those who supply or demand loanable funds, it is also necessary to recognize the underlying economic forces that cause a change in either the supply of or the demand for loanable funds. The following economic factors influence this supply and demand and thereby influence interest rates.

a. **Impact of Economic Growth on Interest Rates**

Changes in economic conditions cause a shift in the demand curve for loanable funds, which affects the equilibrium interest rate. Just as economic growth puts upward pressure on interest rates, an economic slowdown puts downward pressure on the equilibrium interest rate.

When businesses anticipate that economic conditions will improve, they are willing to borrow more funds. Their willingness to borrow more funds at any given interest rate reflects an outward shift (to the right) in the demand curve. The supply-of-loanable-funds schedule may also change in response to economic growth; it is possible that the increased expansion by businesses will lead to more income for construction crews and others who service the expansion. In this case, the quantity of savings (loanable funds supplied) could increase regardless of the interest rate, causing an outward shift in the supply schedule.

b. **Impact of Inflation on Interest Rates**

Changes in inflationary expectations can affect interest rates by affecting the amount of spending by households or businesses. Decisions to spend affect the amount saved (supply of funds) and the amount borrowed (demand for funds). Assume the inflation rate is expected to increase. Households that supply funds may reduce their savings at any interest rate level so that they can make more purchases now before prices rise. This shift in behaviour is reflected by an inward shift (to the left) in the supply curve of loanable funds. In addition, households and businesses may be willing to borrow more funds at any interest rate level so that they can purchase products now before prices increase. This is reflected by an outward shift (to the right) in the demand curve for loanable funds.

c. **Impact of Monetary Policy on Interest Rates**

The National Bank can affect the supply of loanable funds by increasing or reducing the total amount of deposits held at commercial banks or other depository institutions. The process by which the Federal Reserve (Fed) adjusts the money supply. When the Fed increases the money supply, it increases the supply of loanable funds and this places downward pressure on interest rates. If the Fed reduces the money supply, it reduces the supply of loanable funds. Assuming no change in demand, this action places upward pressure on interest rate.

The credit crisis intensified during the fall of 2008, and economic conditions weakened. The Fed increased the money supply in the banking system as a means of ensuring that funds were available for households or businesses that wanted to borrow funds. Consequently, financial institutions had more funds available that they could lend. The increase in the supply of loanable funds placed downward pressure on interest rates. Because the demand for loanable funds decreased during this period (as explained previously), the downward pressure on interest rates was even more pronounced. Interest rates declined substantially in the fall of 2008 in response to these two forces. Since the economy remained weak even after the credit crisis, the Fed continued its policy of injecting funds into the banking system during the 2009–2013 period in order to keep interest rates (the cost of borrowing) low. Its policy was intended to encourage corporations and households to borrow and spend money, in order to stimulate the economy.

d. Impact of the Budget Deficit on Interest

Rates when the federal government enacts fiscal policies that result in more expenditures than tax revenue, the budget deficit are increased. Because of large budget deficits in recent years, the U.S. government is a major participant in the demand for loanable funds. A higher federal government deficit increases the quantity of loanable funds demanded at any prevailing interest rate, which causes an outward shift in the demand curve. Assuming that all other factors are held constant, interest rates will rise. Given a finite amount of loanable funds supplied to the market (through savings), excessive government demand for these funds tends to "crowd out" the private demand (by consumers and corporations) for funds. The federal government may be willing to pay whatever is necessary to borrow these funds, but the private sector may not. This impact is known as the **crowding-out effect**. Flow of funds between the federal government and the private sector. There is a counterargument that the supply curve might shift outward if the government creates more jobs by spending more funds than it collects from the public (this is what causes the deficit in the first place). If this were to occur, then the deficit might not place upward pressure on interest rates.

Much research has investigated this issue and has generally shown that, when holding other factors constant, higher budget deficits place upward pressure on interest rates.

Flow of funds between the federal government and the private sector.

e. Impact of Foreign Flows of Funds on Interest Rates

The *interest rate* for a specific currency is determined by the demand for funds denominated in *that currency* and the supply of funds available in that currency. In recent years, massive flows of funds have shifted between countries, causing abrupt adjustments in the supply of funds available in each country and thereby affecting interest rates. In general, the shifts are driven by large institutional investors seeking a high return on their investments. These investors commonly attempt to invest funds in debt securities in countries where interest rates are high. However, many countries that typically have relatively high interest rates also tend to have high inflation, which can weaken their local currencies. Since the depreciation (decline in value) of a currency can more than offset a high interest rate in some cases, investors tend to avoid investing in countries with high interest rates if the threat of inflation is very high.

Chapter Four: - Financial Markets in the Financial System

Leaning Objectives

At the end of the chapter students/learners will be able to.

- Understand the Organization and Structures of Market
  - Distinguish Primary and Secondary Market
  - Differentiate money and Capital Market
- Recognize Foreign Exchange and Derivative Market

Introduction

A Market is an institutional mechanism where supply and demand will meet to exchange goods and services; or a place or event at which people gather in order to buy and sell things in order to trade. In modern economies, households provide labor, management skills, and natural resources to business firms and governments in return for income in the form of wages, rents and dividends. Consequently, one can see that markets are used to carry out the task of allocating resources which are scarce relative to the demand of the society. Along with many different functions, the financial system fulfills its various roles mainly through markets where financial claims and financial services are traded (though in some least-developed economies Government dictation and even barter are used). These markets may be viewed as channels which move a vast flow of loan able funds that are continually being drawn upon by demanders of funds and continually being replenished by suppliers of funds.

1. *Organization and Structure of Markets*

Broadly speaking, markets can be classified in to Factor markets, Product market and financial markets.

a. *Factor markets*: - are markets where consuming units sell their labor, management skill, and other resources to those producing units offering the highest prices, i.e. this market allocates factors of production (Land, labor and capital – and distribute incomes in the form of wages, rental income and so on to the owners of productive resources.

b. *Product market*: - are markets where consuming units use most of their income from the factor markets to purchase goods and *services* i.e. this market includes the trading of all goods and services that the economy produces at a particular point in time.

c. *A financial market*: - is a market where funds are transferred from people who have an excess of available funds to people who have a shortage. Financial markets such as the bond and stock markets are important in channeling funds from people who do not have a productive use for them to those who do.

d. *Commodity Market*: - a market where primary and secondary commodities are traded. Primary commoditiesare either extracted or captured/harvested/directly from natural resources and requires minimal processing before being used. Secondary commoditiesare produced from primary commodities to satisfy specific market needs. And these commodities also further classified as perishable (soft) commodities and non-perishable (hard) commodities.

i. Organized Exchanges (Auction) Markets

An auction market is some form of centralized facility (or clearing house) by which buyers and sellers, through their commissioned agents (brokers), execute trades in an open and competitive bidding process. The "centralized facility" is not necessarily a place where buyers and sellers physically meet. Rather, it is any institution that provides buyers and sellers with a centralized access to the bidding process. All of the needed information about offers to buy (bid prices) and offers to sell (asked prices) is centralized in one location which is readily accessible to all would-be buyers and sellers, e.g., through a computer network. An auction market is typically a public market in the sense that it open to all agents who wish to participate. Auction markets can either be call markets -- such as art auctions -- for which bid and asked prices are all posted at one time, or continuous markets -- such as stock exchanges and real estate markets -- for which bid and asked prices can be posted at any time the market is open and exchanges take place on a continual basis. Experimental economists have devoted a tremendous amount of attention in recent years to auction markets.

ii. Over-the-counter (OTC) markets

An over-the-counter market has no centralized mechanism or facility for trading. Instead, the market is a public market consisting of a number of dealers spread across a region, a country, or indeed the world, who make the market in some type of asset. That is, the dealers themselves post bid and asked prices for this asset and then stand ready to buy or sell units of this asset with anyone who chooses to trade at these posted prices. The dealers provide customers more flexibility in trading than brokers, because dealers can offset imbalances in the demand and supply of assets by trading out of their own accounts. Many well-known common stocks are traded over-the-counter through NASDAQ (National Association of Securities Dealers' Automated Quotation System). The difference between organized exchange markets and over the counter markets lays on the following issues.

Basis for Comparison

Exchange

OTC (Over the Counter)

Meaning

Exchange is an organized and regulated market, wherein trading of stocks takes place between buyers and sellers in a safe, transparent and systematic manner.

Over the Counter or OTC is a decentralized dealer market wherein brokers and dealers transact directly via computer networks and phone.

Market maker

Exchange itself

Dealer

Used by

Well established companies

Small companies

Physical Location

Yes

No

Trading hours

Exchange hours

24×7

Stocks

Listed Stocks

Unlisted Stocks

Transparency

Comparatively high

Low

Contracts

Standardized

Customized

2. *Primary and secondary market*

Primary Market

It is a financial market in which new issues of a security such as a bond or stock are sold to initial buyers by the corporation or government agency borrowing the funds. The primary markets for securities are not well known to the public because the selling of securities to the initial buyers takes place behind closed doors. An important financial institution that assists in the initial sale of securities in the primary market is the investment bank. It does this by under writing securities: It guarantees a price for a corporation's securities and then sells them to the public.

Secondary Market

It is a financial market in which securities that have been previously issued (and are thus second handed) can be resold.

When an individual buys a security in the secondary market, the person who has sold the security receives money in exchange for the security, but the corporation that issued the security acquires no new funds. A Corporation acquires new funds only when its securities are first sold in the primary market. Nonetheless, secondary market serves two important functions:

1. They make it easier to sell these financial instruments to raise cash; that is, they make the financial instruments more liquid. The increased liquidity of these instruments then makes them more desirable and thus easier for the issuing firm to sell in the primary market.
2. They determine the price of the security that the issuing firm sells in the primary market. The firms that buy securities in the primary market will pay the issuing company no more than the price that they think the secondary market will set for this security. The higher the security's price in the secondary market, the higher will be the price that the issuing firm will receive for a new security in the primary market and hence the greater the amount of capital it can raise. Conditions in the secondary market are therefore the most relevant to corporations issuing securities. It is for this reason that books, which deal with financial markets, focus on the behavior of secondary markets rather than primary markets.

3. *Money Market*

Money market instruments are defined as securities that when issued have a year or less to maturity, and the market that trades in such instruments is known as the money market. Examples of money market instruments are *Treasury bills*, *commercial paper*, *bankers' acceptances*, *certificates of deposit* and *Eurocurrency deposits*. The money market is important because many of these instruments are held by banks as part of their eligible reserves, that is, they may be used (are eligible) as collateral if a bank wishes to raise funds from the central bank.

The money market is itself divided into two interrelated parts, *the domestic money market* and the *international money market*. The domestic market deals with short-term domestic currency deposits that are held in the country of issue. The international money market consists of national currencies that are held on short-term deposit in countries other than the country of issue of that currency. The international money market is referred to as the offshore market or Eurocurrency market.

The money market is a financial market in which only short term debt instruments (maturity of less than one year) are traded. Money market securities, which are discussed in detail latter, have the following characteristics.

- They are usually sold in large denominations
- They have low default risk
- They have smaller fluctuation in prices than long- term securities, making them safer investments
- Widely traded than long- term securities and so more liquid.

Money market transactions do not take place in any one particular location or building. Instead, traders usually arrange purchases and sales between participants over the phone and complete them electronically. Because of this characteristic, money market securities usually have an active *secondary market*. This means that after the security has been sold initially, it is relatively easy to find buyers who will purchase it in the future. An active secondary market makes the money market securities very flexible instruments to use to fill short term financial needs.

Another characteristic of the money markets is that they are **whole- markets.** This means that most transactions are very large. The size of this transaction prevents most individual investors from participating directly in the money markets. Instead, dealers and brokers, operating in the trading rooms of large banks and brokerage houses, bring customers together.

Purposes of the Money Market

The well-developed secondary market for money market instruments makes the money market an ideal place for a firm or financial institution to" warehouse" surplus funds until they are needed. Similarly, the money markets provide a low cost source of funds to firms, the government, and intermediaries that need short term infusion of funds.

Most investors in the money market who are temporarily warehousing funds are ordinarily not trying to earn unusually high returns on their money market funds. Rather, they use the money market as an interim investment that provides a higher return than holding cash or money in banks. They may feel that market conditions are not right to warrant the purchase of additional stock, or they may expect interest rates to rise and hence not want to purchase bonds. It is important to keep in mind that holding idle surplus cash is expensive for an investor because cash balances earn no income for the owner. Idle cash represents an opportunity cost in terms of lost interest income. The money market provides a means to invest idle funds and to reduce this opportunity cost.

Investment advisors often hold funds in the money market so that they will be able to act quickly to take advantage of investment opportunities they indentify. Most investment funds and financial intermediaries also hold money market securities to meet investment or deposit outflows.

The sellers of money market securities find that money market provides a low-cost source of temporary funds. For example, government tax revenues usually come only after certain times of the year, but expenses are incurred all year long. Hence, the government can borrow short term funds that it will pay back when it receives tax revenues. Businesses also face problems caused by revenues and expenses occurring at different times. The money markets provide an efficient, low cost way of solving these problems.

a. **Treasury bills** are issued by the Treasury of the country concerned, and they are generally regarded to be risk-free instruments since the government guarantees to pay their face value upon maturity, and since it can simply print the money to do this they are free of default risk. Another attractive feature of Treasury bills is that they are a highly liquid instrument with a well-developed secondary market which means that holders can easily convert their bills into cash if the need arises. A Treasury bill is a discount security, that is, upon issue the security is sold at a discount to its face value. Since a bill makes no coupon payments, the holder expects to gain from capital appreciation. The size of the discount determines the yield on holding the Treasury bill.

The current yield on a Treasury bill (assuming a 360-day year) is calculated as follows:-

$$Y = \underline{D} \text{ x } \underline{360}$$

$$P \text{ t}$$

Where **Y** is the annualized yield, **D** is the discount to face value (that is the difference between the price and face value), **P** is the current market price, and **t** is the number of days remaining to maturity.

<u>**For example**</u>, on issue a six-month (180-day) Treasury bill with a face value of £100 is sold at £95. The current yield is calculated as:

Solutions

$$Y = 5/95 \text{ x } 360/180 = \underline{\mathbf{10.52\%}}$$

Text Box: $Y = D \text{ x } 360 \text{ P t}$ Where Y is the annualized yield, D is the discount to face value (that is the difference between the price and face value), P is the current market price, and t is the number of days remaining to maturity. For example, on issue a six-month (180-day) Treasury bill with a face value of £100 is sold at £95. The current yield is calculated as: Solutions $Y = 5/95 \text{ x } 360/180 = 10.52\%$

b. **Commercial paper:** - A company that wishes to raise money for short-term purposes might obtain a bank overdraft. Alternatively, if the company has a good credit rating it could issue commercial paper. Commercial paper is an unsecured promissory note issued by a corporation into the money market. The issuer promises to pay purchasers of the issue the face value of the paper which is sold at a discount on the market. Most commercial paper is of less than 360 days to maturity, and the typical maturity range is 30-60 days. The commercial paper market has grown enormously in the United States such that it is now bigger than the US Treasury bill market. In the United States, most commercial paper is paid off by the issue of new commercial paper, and many banks hold commercial paper as part of their eligible assets to meet reserve requirements. The main risk faced by a holder of commercial paper is that the issuer will not be in a position to issue further paper upon maturity, but this risk is kept low by the fact that most commercial paper is backed up by the corporation's access to bank credit facilities. Issuers of commercial paper are also given credit ratings by credit-rating agencies. A large proportion of commercial paper is issued by financial corporations who use the commercial paper market to raise funds to provide loans to customers. Some of these financial corporations are known as captive finance companies, which are basically a subsidiary of a major corporation. The aim of the subsidiary is to raise and manage funds for the parent corporation; for example, in the United States the General Motors Acceptance Corporation issues commercial paper on behalf of General Motors. The commercial paper market was originally used only by corporations that had an excellent credit rating, but in recent years corporations with lower credit ratings have been able to enter the market. They have managed to sell their commercial paper by issuing paper that is backed by a letter of credit from a bank, in which the bank guarantees the commercial paper in the event of default by the issuer. In return for this the bank receives a fee from the issuer. Commercial paper is either placed directly with the investor (direct paper), or is dealer-placed with investors (dealer paper) in return for an underwriting fee. Most direct paper is placed by financial corporations that are raising sufficient amounts of funds on a regular basis to justify the costs of maintaining a sales-force for their paper. Like Treasury bills, commercial paper is sold at a discount to face value based on a 360-day year. One interesting difference between the Treasury bill market and the commercial paper market is that most commercial paper is held to maturity, meaning that the secondary market in commercial paper is relatively thin compared to the high liquidity of the Treasury bill market. The discount on commercial paper is higher than the discount on Treasury bills principally due to the default risk involved and the fact that the secondary commercial paper market is less liquid than the

Treasury bill market.

c. **The interbank market**: - The interbank market is where commercial and investment/merchant banks (both domestic and foreign) as well as other non-bank financial intermediaries can lend and borrow money with each other. Banks with surplus funds can lend to banks which are short of funds. The market is predominantly a short-term market with most loans ranging from overnight loans to 14-day loans, on a much lesser scale some loans are for periods up to six months. The key rate of interest is the London Inter-Bank Offer Rate (LIBOR), which is the rate charged on loans in the market. This forms the basis for the rates banks will charge for loans since it represents the likely cost of funds if they themselves are short of funds. Many variable-rate loan contracts are linked to LIBOR plus a margin.

d. **Bankers' acceptances:** - A banker's acceptance is simply a financial instrument that facilitates a commercial trade transaction. The financial instrument is called a banker's acceptance because a bank will guarantee the repayment of a loan to the holder. They are mainly used to facilitate trade of goods between companies of different countries, although they are occasionally used to facilitate trade between two companies within the same country. Bankers' acceptances help a country to export goods to, and import goods from, the rest of the world. In addition, third-country acceptances are used to finance storing and shipping of goods between two foreign firms.

e. **Repurchase agreements:** - A repurchase agreement involves the sale of a security with a commitment by the seller to repurchase the security at a specified price at a future date. In effect, a repurchase agreement is a collateralized loan with the seller handing over the security as collateral. There are three types of repo maturity.

> P. Overnight repo-it refers one day maturity transaction.
> P. Term repo-refers to a repo with specified end date.
> P. Open repo-simply has no end date.

The yield on repurchase agreements is calculated as the annualized percentage difference between the initial selling price of the securities and the contracted (re)purchase price (the selling price plus interest paid on the repurchase agreement), using a 360-day year.

Specifically:-

$$irepo,sp = \frac{P_f - P_0}{P_0 n} \times 360$$

Where

P_f = Repurchase price of the securities (equals the selling price plus interest paid on

the repurchase agreement)

P_0 = Selling price of the securities

n = Number of days until the repo matures

Illustrative example: - Suppose a bank enters a reverse repurchase agreement in which it agrees to buy fed funds from one of its correspondent banks at a price of $10,000,000, with the promise to sell these funds back at a price of $10,000,291.67 ($10,000,000 plus interest of $291.67) after five days. The yield on this repo to the bank is calculated as follows:

$$irepo, sp = \underline{291.67} \times \underline{360} = \underline{\textbf{0.21\%}}$$

10,000,000 5

f. **Certificate of deposit (CD):-** is issued by a deposit-taking institution, usually a bank, to acknowledge that a specified sum of money has been deposited with the institution. They have a specified maturity date and attract a specified rate of interest. Certificates of deposit come in two forms, negotiable and nonnegotiable. A negotiable CD can be sold by the initial depositor on the open market before maturity, whilst non-negotiable CD must be held by the depositor until maturity. The vast majority of certificates of deposit are issued with less than a year to maturity, with three and six-month deposits being the most common types, and there are also longer-term certificates of deposit issued for periods of one to five years known as term CDs, which pay interest semi-annually. Many term CDs are of the floating rate variety in which the rate of interest varies from time to time in accordance with changes in the base rate of interest.

The international money market is the market in which borrowers and lenders of funds from different countries are brought together to exchange funds.

The main international money market is known as the Eurocurrency market, and since the early 1960s this market has grown at an astonishing pace. As we shall see, the development of the Eurocurrency market has had important implications for not only the international monetary system, but also for the development of domestic financial markets and the conduct of national macroeconomic policies.

The Eurocurrency market and the Eurobond market. Eurocurrency markets are defined as banking markets which involve short-term borrowing and lending conducted outside of the legal jurisdiction of the authorities of the currency that is used; for example Eurodollar deposits are dollar deposits held in London and Paris. The Eurocurrency market has two sides to it; the receipt of deposits and the loaning out of those deposits. By far the most important Eurocurrency is the Eurodollar which currently accounts for approximately 65-70 per cent of all Eurocurrency activity, followed by the Euromark, Eurofrancs (Swiss), Eurosterling and Euroyen. The use of the prefix Euro is somewhat misleading because dollar deposits held by banks in Hong Kong or Tokyo are equally outside the legal jurisdiction of the US authorities and also constitute Eurodollar deposits. This more widespread geographical base means that Euromarkets are often referred to as 'offshore' markets.

4. *Capital Market*

The Capital Market

The last topic discussed short-term securities that trade in a market we call the ***money market***. This topic will discuss about the first of several securities that trade in a market we call the ***capital market***. Capital markets are for securities with an original maturity that is greater than one year. These securities include ***bonds***, ***stocks***, and ***mortgages***. We will devote to each major type of capital market security due to their importance to investors, businesses, and the economy.

Capital market is a financial market for **debt** and **equity** instruments with maturities of greater than one year. They have far wider price fluctuations than money market instruments and are considered to be fairly risky investments.

Firms that issue capital securities and the investors who buy them have very different motivations than those who operate in the money markets. Firms and individuals use the money markets primarily to *warehouse funds* for short period of time until a more important need or a more productive use for the funds arises. To the contrary, firms and individuals use the capital markets for long term investments.

The primary issuers of capital market securities are federal and local governments and corporations. The federal government issues long-term notes and bonds to fund the national debt. State and municipal governments also issue long-term notes and bonds to finance capital projects, such as school and prison construction. *Governments never issue stock* because they cannot sell ownership claims.

Corporations issue both bonds and stock. One of the most difficult decisions a firm faces can be whether it should finance its growth with debt or equity. The distribution of a firm's capital between debt and equity is called its capital structure. Corporations may enter the capital markets because they do not have sufficient capital to fund their investment opportunities. Alternatively, firms may choose to enter the capital markets because they want to preserve their capital to protect against unexpected needs. In either case, the availability of efficiently functioning capital markets is crucial to the continued health of the business sector. This was dramatically demonstrated during the 2008–2009 financial crises. With the near collapse of the bond and stock markets, funds for business expansion dried up. This led to reduced business activity, high unemployment, and slow growth. Only after market confidence was restored did a recovery begin.

Capital market trading occurs in either the primary market or the secondary market. The primary market is where new issues of stocks and bonds are introduced. When firms sell securities for the very first time, the issue is an initial public offering (IPO). Subsequent sales of a firm's new stocks or bonds to the public are simply primary market transactions (as opposed to an initial one).

The capital markets have well-developed secondary markets. A secondary market is where the sale of previously issued securities takes place. Secondary markets are critical in capital markets because most investors plan to sell long-term bonds at some point before they mature. There are two types of exchanges in the secondary market for capital securities: *organized exchanges* and *over-the-counter* exchanges.

4.4.1. Debt Market

Firm or an individual can obtain funds in a financial market in two ways. The most common method is to issue a debt instrument, such as a bond or a mortgage, which is a contractual agreement by the borrower to pay the holder of the instrument fixed Birr amounts at regular intervals (interest and principal payments) until a specified date (the maturity date), when a final payment is made. The maturity of a debt instrument is the number of years (term) until that instrument's expiration date.

Types of Bonds

Bonds are securities that represent a debt owed by the issuer to the investor. Bonds obligate the issuer to pay a specified amount at a given date, generally with periodic interest payments. The par, face, or maturity value of the bond (they all mean the same thing) is the amount that the issuer must pay at maturity. The **coupon rate** is the rate of interest that the issuer must pay, and this periodic interest payment is often called the coupon payment. This rate is usually fixed for the duration of the bond and does not fluctuate with market interest rates. If the repayment terms of a bond are not met, the holder of a bond has a claim on the assets of the issuer.

Long-term bonds traded in the capital market include long-term *government notes and bonds, municipal bonds*, and *corporate bonds.*

a. **Treasury Notes and Bonds:** - The U.S. Treasury issues notes and bonds to finance the national debt. The differencebetween a note and a bond is that notes have an original maturity of 1 to10 years while bonds have an original maturity of 10 to 30 years. Federal **government treasury notes and bonds** are free of default risk because the government can always print money to pay off the debt if necessary. This does *not* mean that these securities are risk-free.

b. **Municipal Bonds:** - Municipal bonds are securities issued by local, county, and state governments. Theproceeds from these bonds are used to finance public interest projects, such asschools, utilities, and transportation systems. Interest earned on municipal bondsthat are issued to pay for essential public projects are exempt from federal taxation. Because investors will be satisfied with lower interest rates on tax-exempt bonds. **<u>Illustrative example</u>**: - Suppose that the interest rate on a taxable corporate bond is 5% and that the marginal tax is 28%. Suppose a tax-free municipal bond with a rate of 3.75% was available. Which security would you choose?

<u>Solution</u>

The tax-free equivalent municipal interest rate is 3.6%.

Equivalent tax free rate = taxable interest rate * (1 - marginal tax rate)

where

Taxable interest rate = 0.05

Marginal tax rate = 0.28

Thus,

Equivalent tax free rate = 0.05 * (1 - .28) = 0.036 = **<u>3.6%</u>**

Since the tax-free municipal bond rate (3.75%) is higher than the equivalent tax-free rate (3.6%), choose the municipal bond.

There are *two types* of municipal bonds: *general obligation* bonds and *revenue bonds.* General obligation bonds do not have specific assets pledged as security or a specific source of revenue allocated for their repayment. Instead, they are backed by the "full faith and credit" of the issuer. This phrase means that the issuer promises to use every resource available to repay the bond as promised. Most general obligation bond issues must be approved by the taxpayers because the taxing authority of the government is pledged for their repayment. Revenue bonds, by contrast, are backed by the cash flow of a particular revenue-generating project.

Municipal bonds are not default-free. Default rates are higher during periods when the economy is weak. Clearly, governments are not exempt from financial distress. Unlike the federal government, local governments cannot print money, and there are real limits on how high they can raise taxes without driving the population away.

c. **Corporate Bonds:** - When large corporations need to borrow funds for long periods of time, they may issue bonds. Most corporate bonds have a face value of $1,000 and pay interest semiannually (twice per year). Most are also callable, meaning that the issuer may redeem the bonds prior to maturity after a specified date. The **bond indenture** is a contract that states the lender's rights and privileges and the borrower's obligations. Any collateral offered as security to the bondholders is also described in the indenture. The degree of risk varies widely among different bond issues because the risk of default depends on the company's health, which can be affected by a number of variables. The interest rate on corporate bonds varies with the level of risk.

d. **Mortgages:** - is a debt issued to purchase real estate, such as a house or condo. It is a form of secured debt as the subject real estate is used as collateral against the loan. They offer prime and subprime mortgages. For prime the home serves as collateral in the event that the borrower is not able to make the mortgage payments. Subprime borrowers who do not have sufficient income to qualify for prime mortgages or who are unable to make a down payment. However, mortgages are so unique that they deserve their own debt classification.

4.4.2. Equity Market

A share of stock in a firm represents ownership. A stockholder owns a percentage interest in a firm, consistent with the percentage of outstanding stock held. Investors can earn a return from stock in one of two ways. Either the price of the stock rises over time or the firm pays the stockholder dividends. Frequently, investors earn a return from both sources. Stock is riskier than bonds because stockholders have a lower priority than bondholders when the firm is in trouble, dividends are less assured, and stock price increases are not guaranteed. Despite these risks, it is possible to make a great deal of money by investing in stock, whereas that is very unlikely by investing in bonds. Another distinction between stock and bonds is that stock does not mature.

Ownership of stock gives the stockholder certain rights regarding the firm. One is the right of a residual claimant: Stockholders have a claim on all assets and income left over after all other claimants have been satisfied. If nothing is left over, they get nothing. As noted, however, it is possible to get rich as a stockholder if the firm does well. Most stockholders have the right to vote for directors and on certain issues, such as amendments to the corporate charter and whether new shares should be issued.

i. **Common stock:** -The fundamental ownership claim in a public or private corporation.

Common stock, as an investment has the following basic characteristic features

F. *Residual claim* means stockholders are the last in line of all those who have a claim on the assets and income of the corporation. In a liquidation of the firm's assets, the shareholders have claim to what is left after paying all other claimants, such as tax authorities, employees, suppliers, bondholders, and other creditors. In a going concern, shareholders have claim to the part of operating income left after interest and taxes have been paid. Management either can pay this residual as cash dividends to shareholders or reinvest it in the business to increase the value of the shares.

F. *Limited liability* means that the most shareholders can lose in the event of the failure of the corporation is their original investment. Shareholders are not like owners unincorporated businesses, whose creditors can lay claim to the personal assets of the owner. In the event of the firm's bankruptcy corporate stock holders at worst have worthless stock. They are not personally liable for the firm's obligations: Their liability is limited.

F. *Voting Right:* Each share of a common stock provides the holder with one vote in the election of board of directors and on other decision making activities.

F. *Dividends:* Payment of dividends to shareholders is at the corporation's board of directors discretion

F. *Pre-emptive Rights:* Allows common stock holders to maintain their proportionate ownership in the corporation when new shares are issued.

ii. **Preferred stock:** - is a form of equity from a legal and tax standpoint. However, it differs from common stock in several important ways. First, because preferred stockholders receive a fixed dividend that never changes, a share of preferred stock is as much like a bond as it is like common stock. Second, because the dividend does not change, the price of preferred stock is relatively stable. Third, preferred stockholders do not usually vote unless the firm has failed to pay the promised dividend.

Finally, preferred stockholders hold a claim on assets that has priority over the claims of common shareholders but after that of creditors such as bondholders. This may be because preferred dividends are not tax-deductible to the firm like bond interest payments. Consequently, preferred stock usually has a higher cost than debt, even though it shares many of the characteristics of a bond.

Basis of Difference

Money Market

Capital Market

Definitions

It is the part of financial market where lending and borrowing takes place for short-term up to one year

Capital market is part of the financial market where lending and borrowing takes place for the medium-term and long-term

Types of instruments

Money market instruments are treasury bills, commercial bills, certificates of deposits, and other short-period securities.

Capital market instruments are equity shares, preference shares, debentures, bonds, and other long-period securities.

Institutions involved

The money market contains, the central bank, commercial banks, financial companies, money market mutual funds governments, corporations, brokers and dealers

It involves stockbrokers, mutual funds, underwriters, individual investors, commercial banks, stock exchanges, Insurance Companies

Liquidity of the market

Money markets are liquid

Capital Markets are comparatively less liquid

Maturity

Short term less than a year.

Medium to long term more than a year

Risk factor

Since the market is liquid and the maturity is less than one year, Risk involved is low

Due to less liquid nature and long maturity, the risk is comparatively high

Functional merit

The money markets increase the liquidity of funds in the economy

The capital market stabilizes the economy due to long-term savings

5. *Foreign Exchange Markets*

In an open economy that trade with one another, there is a major difference in the transactions between domestic and foreign residents as compared to those between residents of the same country, namely, that differing national currencies are usually involved. A US importer will generally have to pay a Japanese exporter in yen, a German exporter in deutschmarks and a British exporter in pounds. For this reason, the US importer will have to buy these currencies with dollars in what is known as the foreign exchange market. *The foreign exchange market is not a single physical place, rather it is defined as a market where the various national currencies are bought and sold. The foreign exchange market is where the various national currencies are bought and sold.* One of the most fascinating things about the foreign exchange market is the huge sums of money that are exchanged on a daily basis.

The exchange rate is simply the price of one currency in terms of another, and may therefore be expressed in either of two ways:-

- *Foreign currency units per unit of the domestic currency*; for example taking the pound sterling as the domestic currency, on 11 August 2004, $1.8277 dollars were required to obtain one pound that is $1.8277 /£1. ....December 08, 2022 -----$1/54 Birr
- *Domestic currency units per unit of foreign currency*; for example, taking the pound sterling as the domestic currency on 11 August 2004 approximately £0.5471 was required to purchase one US dollar, that is £0.54 71/$1. ......December 08, 2022--- 0.019 Birr/1$

Obviously the second method is merely the reciprocal of the former. While it is not important which method of expressing the exchange rate is employed, it is necessary to be careful when talking about a rise or fall in the exchange rate because the meaning will be very different depending upon which definition is used. A rise in the pounds per dollar exchange rate from say £0.55/$1 to £0.60/$1 means that more pounds have to be given to obtain a dollar, which means that the pound has depreciated in value, or equivalently the dollar has appreciated in value. If the first definition is employed, a rise in the dollars per pound exchange rate from $1.83/£1 to $1.90/£1 would mean that more dollars are obtained per pound, so that the pound has appreciated or equivalently the dollar has depreciated.

The foreign exchange market is a worldwide market and is made up primarily of commercial banks, foreign exchange brokers and other authorized agents trading in most of the currencies of the world. These groups are kept in close and continuous contact with one another and with developments in the market via telephone, computer terminals, telex and fax. Among the most important foreign exchange centers are London, New York, Tokyo, Singapore and Frankfurt.

One of the most important implications deriving from the close communication of buyers and sellers in the foreign exchange market is that there is almost instantaneous arbitrage across currencies and financial centers. Arbitrage is the exploitation of price differentials for riskless guaranteed profits.

Foreign exchange dealers not only deal with a wide variety of currencies but they also have a set of dealing rates for each currency which are known as the **spot** and **forward rates**.

- **Spot rates:** - The spot exchange rate is the quotation between two currencies for *immediate delivery*. In other words, the spot exchange rate is the current exchange rate of two currencies *vis-a-vis* each other.
- **Forward exchange rate:**- In addition to the spot exchange rate, it is possible for economic agents to agree today to exchange currencies at some specified time in the *future*, most commonly 1 month (30 days), 3 months (90 days), 6 months (180 days), 9 months (270 days) or 1 year (360 days) hence. The rate of exchange at which such a purchase or sale can be made is known as the forward exchange rate.

6. *The Derivative Market*

Derivative: - is a contract between *two or more people* whose value is based on an underlying asset. The underlying assets are financial instruments such as stocks, bonds, treasury bills, foreign currencies and commodities.

The instruments that can be used to provide such protection are called *derivative instruments*. The term derivatives refers to a large number of financial instruments, the value of which is based on, or derived from, the prices of securities, commodities, money or other external variables.

Functions of Derivatives

- *Discovery of price:* - derivatives help in discovery of future as well as current prices(DD=SS).
- *Risk transfer:* - helps to transfer risks from those who have them to those who have an appetite for them.
- *Linked to cash markets:* - underlying market witnesses higher trading volumes because of participation by more players.
- *Check on speculation*: - Speculation traders shift to a more controlled environment of the derivatives market.

- **Encourages entrepreneurship:-** An important incidental benefit that flows from derivatives trading is that it acts as a catalyst for new entrepreneurial activity. Derivatives have a history of attracting many bright, creative, well-educated people with an entrepreneurial attitude. They often energize others to create new businesses, new products and new employment opportunities, the benefit of which are immense.
- **Encourage saving and investments:-** Derivatives markets help increase savings and investment in the long run.

Benefits of Derivatives

- **Risk aversion tools:** - control, avoid, shift and manage efficiently different types of risks through hedging, arbitraging, spreading.
- **Prediction of future prices:** - discovery of new prices both on the spot and futures markets.
- **Enhance liquidity:** - in derivatives trading no immediate full amount of the transaction is required.
- **Assist investors:** - proper asset allocation (portfolio) increases their yields and achieves other investment goals.
- **Integration of price structure:** - derivatives have smoothened out price fluctuations, squeeze the price spreads, integrate price structure at different points of time.
- **Catalyze growth of financial markets:-** derivatives trading encourage the competitive trading in the markets, different risk taking preference of the market operators(1)
- **Brings perfection in market:** - Complete market concept refers to that situation where no particular investors can be better off than others.

The types of derivative contacts include *futures contracts, forward contracts, option contracts*, and *swap* contact agreements.

a. **Spot contract:** - agreement made between a buyer and a seller at time 0 for the seller to deliver the asset immediately and the buyer to pay for the asset immediately.

For example:- A spot bond quote of $97 for a 20-year maturity bond is the price the buyer must pay the seller, per $100 of face value, for immediate (time 0) delivery of the 20-year bond.

Spot transactions occur because the buyer of the asset believes its value will increase in the immediate future (over the investor's holding period). If the value of the asset increases as expected, the investor can sell the asset at its higher price for a profit. For example, if the 20-year bond increases in value to $99 per $100 of face value, the investor can sell the bond for a profit of $2 per $100 of face value.

b. **Forward Contracts:** - is an agreement which allows the holder of the contract to buy or sell a certain asset at or by a certain day at a certain price.

- the certain day—maturity or expiration date,
- the certain price—delivery price,
- the person who write the contract (has the asset) is called in short position,
- the person who holds the contract is called in long position.

Forward contracts on foreign exchange are very popular. Most large banks employ both spot and forward foreign-exchange traders. Spot traders are trading a foreign currency for almost immediate delivery. Forward traders are trading for delivery at a future time. If the forward rate is less than the current spot rate, then forward currency is said to be selling at *a forward discount*. If the forward rate exceeds the current spot rate, then forward currency is selling at *a forward premium*. Forward contracts are sometimes referred to in terms of their percentage premium or discount rather than their actual rate. For example, assume that the spot rate (S) of the Canadian dollar is $0.70 while the 180-day forward rate (FR) is $0.71. The forward rate premium (p) would be

Description: C:\Users\user\Desktop\solution.JPG

This premium simply reflects the percentage by which the forward rate exceeds the spot rate on an annualized basis.

An investor enters into a three month forward contract to sell 100,000 British pounds for US dollars at an exchange rate of 1.5000 US dollars per pound. How much does the investor gain or lose if the exchange rate at the end of the contract is (a) 1.4900 and (b) 1.5200?

(a) The investor is obligated to sell pounds for 1.5000 when they are worth 1.4900. The

gain is (1.5000–1.4900) ×100,000 = **$1,000.**

(b) The investor is obligated to sell pounds for 1.5000 when they are worth 1.5200. The *loss* is (1.5200–1.5000)×100,000 = (**$2,000**)

Features of Forward Contract

- It is bilateral contracts, and hence, they are exposed to counterparty non-performance of obligation by either of the parties.
- Each contract is custom designed (not standardized), and hence, is unique in terms of contract size, expiration date, the asset type, quality, etc.
- There is long position by buyer whereas short positions by seller.
- There is forward and delivery price. Both are equal at the time the contract is entered into. However, as time passes, the forward price is likely to change whereas the delivery price remains the same.
- Assets are oftenly known as synthetic assets in the forward market.
- The contract has to be settled by delivery of the asset on expiration date.

c. **Future Contacts:** - is an agreement between a buyer and a seller at time 0 to exchange a standardized asset for cash at some future date. Each contract has a standardized expiration and transactions occur in a centralized market. The price of the futures contract changes daily as the market value of the asset underlying the futures fluctuates. A futures contract, or simply called futures, is a contract to buy or sell a stated quantity of a commodity or financial instruments at a specified price at a future specified date. The parties to the futures have to buy or sell the asset regardless of what happens to its value during the intervening period or what happens to be the price on the date when the contract is implemented.

- Both the parties to the futures have a right to transfer the contract by entering into an offsetting futures contract.

- If not transferred until the settlement/specified date, then they have obligations to fulfill the terms and conditions of the contract.
  - Futures are traded on the exchanges and the terms of the futures contracts are standardized by the exchange with reference to quantity, date, units of price quotation, minimum change in price.
  - Futures are traded at the organized exchanges only. Some of the centers where futures are traded are Chicago Board of Trade, Tokyo Stock Exchange, London International Financial Futures Exchange (LIFFE), etc. The exchange provides the counter-party guarantee through its clearing house and different types of margins system.
  - Futures contracts are marked to market at the end of each trading day. Fxc, interest rate, bond index

The default risk of a futures contract is less than that of a forward contract for at least four reasons: (1) daily marking to market of futures (so that there is no buildup of losses or gains), (2) margin requirements on futures that act as a security bond should a counterparty default, (3) price movement limits that spread extreme price fluctuations over time, and (4) default guarantees by the futures exchange itself.

Difference b/n Forward and Future Contracts

v. Forward contracts are generally easier to analyze than futures contracts because in forward contracts there is no daily settlement and only a single payment is made at maturity.

Derivative contacts

d. **Options Contracts:** - Option may be definedas a contract between two parties where one gives the other the right (not the obligation) to buy or sell an underlying asset as a specified price within or on a specific time. Option can be ***American*** options that can be exercised *at any time up to the expiration date* and ***European*** options that can be exercised *only on the expiration* date itself. Options also classified as either ***call options*** or ***put options****.*If the contract gives the holder the right to purchase the underlying asset at a predetermined price from the other party the contact is known as ***a call option***. If the contract gives the owner the right to sell the underlying asset at a predetermined price from the other party the contact is known as ***a put option****.*There are basically four types of positions that can be taken on an options contract as follows:

- Buying a call option - known as being long on a call.
- Selling a call option - known as being short on a call.
- Buying a put option - known as being long on a put.
- Selling a put option - known as being short on a put.

- The investor may **_buy a call option_** to secure the right, but not the obligation, to buy a stock at the exercise price (**_buy if price is above the exercise price_**).

Illustrative example:- Consider the situation of an investor who buys a European *call option* with a strike price of 100 to purchase 100 shares of a certain stock. Suppose that the current stock price is $98, the expiration date of the option is in 4 months, and the price of an option to purchase one share is $5. The initial investment is $500. Because the option is European, the ***investor can exercise only on the expiration date***. If the stock price on this date is less than $100, the investor will clearly choose **not to exercise**. (There is no point in buying for $100 a share that has a market value of less than $100). In these circumstances, the investor loses the whole of the initial investment of $500.

v. If the current price at the end of 4 month is a) 90 **b) 115** c) 95 What is the decision? In case of a and c not exercised.

Suppose that the stock price is $115. By exercising the option, the investor is able to buy 100 shares for $100 per share. If the shares are sold immediately, the investor makes a gain of $15 per share, or $1,500, ignoring transaction costs. When the initial cost of the option is taken into account, the net profit to the investor is $1,000.

  v. In general, call options should always be exercised at the expiration date *if the stock*
  v. *price is above the strike price*.

- The company may ***buy a put option*** to secure the right, but not the obligation, to sell stock at the exercise price (sell if the ***price of the stock is below the exercise price***).

Illustrative example: - Consider an investor who buys a European ***put option*** with a strike price of $70 to sell 100 shares of a certain stock.

Suppose that the current stock price is $65, the expiration date of the option is in 3 months, and the price of an option to sell one share is $7. The initial investment is $700. Because the option is European, it will be exercised only if the stock price is below $70 on the expiration date. Suppose that the stock price is a)$55 b)$75.

The investor can buy 100 shares for $55 per share and, under the terms of the put option, sell the same shares for $70 to realize a gain of $15 per share, or $1,500.

When the $700 initial cost of the option is taken into account, the investor's net profit is $800.

There is no guarantee that the investor will make a gain. If the final stock price is above $70, the put option expires worthless, and the investor loses $700.

The purchaser of a ***call option*** is hoping that the stock price will increase, the purchaser of a ***put option*** is hoping that it will decrease.

  v. Buyer of **call options** has the right to buy call option if price **increased**. And Buyer of put option has the right to sell put option if the market price at expiration is below the strike price.

- Note that the investor and company enter into totally different option contracts to manage their risks.

  e. **Swap Contract:** - is an agreement between two parties to exchange two differing forms of payment obligations. Swaps are typically derivatives in which two parties exchange (swap) cash flows or other financial instruments over multiple periods (months or years) for mutual benefit, usually to manage risk. Swaps of this type involve obligations in the future on the part of both parties to the contract. These swaps, like forwards and futures, are forward commitments or bilateral contracts because both parties have a commitment in the future. Similar to forwards and futures, a contract's net initial value to each party should be zero and as one side of the swap contract gains the other side loses by the same amount. Swaps in which two parties exchange cash flows of two kinds: *(i) interest rate swaps*, and *(ii) currency swaps*. In the former the exchange involves payments denominated in the same currency, while in a currency swap the exchange involves two different currencies. Like many other financial instruments, swap agreements are used to manage risk exposure; however, as we shall see, one of the main reasons for the rapid growth of the swap market has been that they enable parties to raise funds more cheaply than would otherwise be the case. The swap markets are used extensively by major corporations, international financial institutions and governments and are an important part of the international bond market. The swap market is currently organized by the International Swap Dealers Association (ISDA) which since 1985 has been responsible for standardizing documentation and dealing terms in the swap market.

Interest rate swap: - An exchange of fixed-interest payments for floating-interest payments by two counterparties. In a swap contract, the swap buyer agrees to make a number of fixed interest rate payments based on a principal contractual amount (called the notional principal) on periodic settlement dates to the swap seller. The swap seller, in turn, agrees to make floating-rate payments, tied to some interest rate, to the swap buyer on the same periodic settlement dates. In undertaking this transaction, the party that is the fixed-rate payer is seeking to transform the variable-rate nature of its liabilities into fixed-rate liabilities to better match the fixed returns earned on its assets. Meanwhile, the party that is the variable-rate payer seeks to turn its fixed[1]rate liabilities into variable-rate liabilities to better match the variable returns on its assets. *Currency swaps:* - is used to hedge against exchange rate risk from mismatched currencies on assets and liabilities. As an example of a currency swap, Company ABC, a US firm, wants to do business in Europe. At the same time, Company XYZ, an European firm, wants to do business in the United States. The US firm needs Euros and the European firm needs Dollars, so the companies enter into a five-year currency swap for $50 million. Assume that the exchange rate is $1.25 per euro. On this basis, Company ABC pays Company XYZ $50 million, and Company XYZ pays €40 million to Company ABC. Now each company has funds denominated in the other currency (which is the reason for the swap). The two companies then exchange monthly, quarterly, or annual interest payments. Finally, at the end of the five-year swap, the parties re-exchange the original principal amounts and the contract ends. The use of swaps has grown because they allow investors to manage many kinds of risks, including interest rate risk, currency risk, and credit default risk. In addition, investors can use swaps to reduce borrowing and transaction costs, overcome currency exchange barriers, and manage exposure to underlying assets.

Chapter Five: - The Regulation of Financial Markets and Institutions

Leaning Objectives

At the end of the chapter students/learners will be able to.

- *Describe the rational why financial institutions regulated*

Text Box: Leaning Objectives At the end of the chapter students/learners will be able to. ü Describe the rational why financial institutions regulated ü Distinguish nature and form of financial system regulation ü Recognize arguments regarding regulation

Introduction

The preceding section showed that financial institutions provide various services to sectors of the economy. Failure to provide these services, or a breakdown in their efficient provision, can be costly to both the ultimate suppliers of funds and users of funds as well as to the economy overall. The financial crisis of the late 2000s is a prime example of how such a breakdown in the provision of financial services can cripple financial markets worldwide and bring the world economy into a deep recession. For example, bank failures may destroy household savings and at the same time restrict a firm's access to credit. Insurance company failures may leave household members totally exposed in old age to the cost of catastrophic illnesses and to sudden drops in income upon retirement. In addition, individual FI failures may create doubts in savers' minds regarding the stability and solvency of FIs and the financial system in general and cause panics and even withdrawal runs on sound institutions.

FIs are regulated in an attempt to prevent these types of market failures and the costs they would impose on the economy and society at large. Although regulation may be socially beneficial, it also imposes private costs, or a regulatory burden, on individual FI owners and managers. Consequently, regulation is an attempt to enhance the social welfare benefits and mitigate the costs of the provision of FI services.

The regulatory structure in the United State is largely the result of financial crises that have occurred at various times. Most regulatory mechanisms are the products of the stock market crash of 1929 and the Great Depression in the 1930s.

Financial institutions are subject to regulation to ensure that they do not take excessive risk and can safely facilitate the flow of funds through financial markets.

Regulation is a rule or order or directive or act or law or ordinance or pronouncement or proclamation made by the government. It can be defined as "A rule of order having the force of law, prescribed by a superior or competent authority, relating to the actions of those under the authority's control.

Financial regulation is a form of regulation or supervision, which subjects financial markets and institutions to certain requirements, restrictions and guidelines, aiming to maintain the integrity of the financial system. This may be handled by either a government or non-government organization or a body established by a government for this purpose.

Regulatory bodies are established by governments or other organizations to oversee the functioning and fairness of financial markets and the firms that engage in financial activity.

1. *Principles of Regulation*

The main principle of the regulation of the financial markets and institutions includes:- *Competitive Neutrality*; *Cost Effectiveness*; *Accountability*; *Flexibility*; and *Transparency*

a. **Competitive Neutrality**

The regulatory burden applying to a particular financial commitment or promise should apply equally to all who make such commitments, as per the competitive neutrality principle. It requires further that there would be:-

- Minimal barriers to entry and exit from markets and products;
- No undue restrictions on institutions or the products they offer; and
- Markets open to the widest possible range of participants.

b. **Cost Effectiveness**

Regulation can be made totally effective by simply prohibiting all actions potentially incompatible with the regulatory objective. But, by inhibiting productive activities along with the anti-social, such an approach is likely to be highly inefficient. Cost effectiveness is one of the most difficult issues for regulatory cultures to come to terms with. Any form of regulation involves a natural tension between effectiveness and efficiency.

Yet the underlying legislative framework must be effective, by fostering compliance through enforcement in cases where participants do not abide by the rules.

- In general, a *cost-effective regulatory* system may requires:

F. an allocation of functions among regulatory bodies which minimizes overlaps, duplication and conflicts;
F. an explicit mandate for regulatory bodies to balance efficiency and effectiveness;
F. the allocation of regulatory costs to those enjoying the benefits; and
F. a presumption in favour of minimal regulation unless a higher level of intervention is justified.

c. **Accountability**

The regulatory structure must be accountable to its stakeholders and subject to regular reviews of its efficiency and effectiveness. In addition, regulatory agencies should operate independently of sectional interests and with appropriately skilled staff.

d. **Flexibility**

The regulatory framework must have the flexibility to cope up with changing institutional and product structures without losing its effectiveness.

e. **Transparency**

Transparency of regulation requires that all guarantees be made explicit and that all purchasers and providers of financial products be fully aware of their rights and responsibilities. It should be a top priority of an effective financial regulatory structure that financial promises (both public and private) to be understood. If there is a general perception that a particular group of financial institutions cannot fail because they have the authorization of government, there is a great danger that perception will become a reality.

2. *Purpose of Regulation*

It is possible that governments may regulate markets that are viewed as competitive currently, but unable to sustain competition, and thus low-cost production, over the long run. A version of this justification for regulation is that the government controls a feature of the economy that the market mechanisms of competition and pricing could not manage without help. A shorthand expression used by economists to describe the reasons for regulation is **market failure**.

i. **Market confidence**: - Financial regulations' main aim is to maintain market confidence. This objective can be achieved by promoting competition and fairness (transparency) in the trading of financial securities. This means that there should be no barriers to entry and exit from markets and financial systems. The market should be open to a wide range of participants who meet specified eligibility criteria. In addition, the markets should provide an effective mechanism for the circulation of securities, the right conditions for investment and promote economic development. The markets are not possible without investors, individuals and entities that have spare cash and want to invest in securities.

ii. **Promote Financial Stability**: - A key objective for financial regulation is to increase the effective functioning of the financial system in order to enhance the ability to absorb or overcome financial instability. There are four main factors that can initiate financial instability: a) increase in interest rates b) increase in uncertainty c) negative shocks to firms' balance sheets d) a deterioration in financial intermediaries' balance sheets. Examples of financial instability a) Asian crisis of second half of 1990 b) U.S. market crisis of 2007 c) European markets crisis of 2010.

iii. **Consumer protection**:- It is the ultimate objective of all of the above of regulations to protect consumers in one or the other way. Some companies may conceal relevant information or give wrong financial picture to attract investments from people and investors. Financial regulations prevent issuers of securities from defrauding investors. Consumer protection also refers to arrangements to protect depositors (or like arrangements for other classes of investors) in the event of the failure of a financial institution to pay their deposits back.

iv. **Reduction of Financial crime**:- Financial regulations also require reducing financial crime of market participants. Various companies and other financial institutions involve in inflating their financial information to attract investments. Companies often involve in illegal insider trading and violation of laws. a) Insider trading: Insider trading is defined as a malpractice wherein trade of a company's securities is undertaken by people who by virtue of their work has access to the otherwise non-public information which can be crucial for making investment decisions. When insiders, e.g. key employees or executives who have access to the strategic information about the company, use the same for trading in the company's stocks or securities, it is called insider trading and it is highly discouraged by the securities exchange commission. Insider trading is an unfair practice, wherein the other stock holders are at great disadvantage due to lack of important insider non-public information.

v. **Regulating foreign participation**: - Especially for under developed countries, regulating foreign participation in the domestic markets may be necessary to protect the financial interests of the country and its economy. In such cases, some countries may restrict activities of foreign concerns in the domestic markets and institutions. Otherwise, these countries may limit the roles of foreign firms on domestic markets and their ownership control of financial institutions.

3. *Nature and Form of Financial System Regulation*

The initial focus, and still the central element, of regulatory system are to solve the problem of the uninformed investor through company disclosure and transparency of trading markets. Most people agree that disclosure provides the information needed to make rational decisions. But regulation today goes far beyond disclosure requirements, because a growing number of stakeholders are presumed to be unskilled and incapable of making informed decisions. For example, because of asymmetric information in financial markets, that means investors may be subject to adverse selection and moral hazard problems that may hinder the efficient operation of financial markets. Risky firms or outright crooks may be the most eager to sell securities to unwary investors, and the resulting adverse selection problem may keep investors out of financial markets. Furthermore, once an investor has bought a security, thereby lending money to a firm, the borrower may have incentives to engage in risky activities or to commit outright fraud. The presence of this moral hazard problem may also keep investors away from financial markets. Government regulation can reduce adverse selection and moral hazard problems in financial markets and increase their efficiency by increasing the amount of information available to investors.

The other basis for financial regulation is concern about *systemic risk*. Systemic risk arises if the failure of one financial institution causes a run on other institutions and precipitates system-wide failure. Regulation is said to be required because individual institutions do not adequately take account of the external costs they impose on the financial system when they fail. But almost every aspect of financial markets, if not daily living itself, involves systemic risk.One of the most complex issues facing governments is identifying the appropriate level and form of intervention.

In similar ways, ensuring the soundness of financial system is the other reason for the necessity of the rules and procedures. Uncertain and confusing information can also lead to widespread collapse of financial intermediaries, referred to as a financial panic. Because providers of funds to financial intermediaries may not be able to assess whether the institutions holding their funds are sound, if they have doubts about the overall health of financial intermediaries, they may want to pull their funds out of both sound and unsound institutions.

Regulatory efficiency is a significant factor in the overall performance of the economy. Inefficiency ultimately imposes costs on the community through higher taxes and charges, poor service, uncompetitive pricing or slower economic growth. The possible outcome is a financial panic that produces large losses for the public and causes serious damage to the economy.

The financial system is regulated to increase the information available to investors, to ensure the soundness of the financial system and improve control of monetary policy.

To protect the public and the economy from financial panics, the governments are implementing a number of regulations. These regulations are have different nature and taking different **form** that includes: - ***Restrictions on Entry; Disclosure regulation, Restrictions of financial institutions, Deposit Insurance,***

a. **Restrictions on Entry:**-Governments endorse very tight regulations governing who is allowed to set up a financial intermediary. Individuals or groups that want to establish a financial intermediary, such as a bank or an insurance company, must obtain a charter from the state or the Federal Government.

b. **Disclosure Regulation:**-There are stringent reporting requirements for financial intermediaries. Their bookkeeping must follow certain strict principles, their books are subject to periodic inspection, and they must make certain information available to the public.

c. **Regulation of financial institutions:**-It is also called regulations on assets and activities. There are restrictions on what financial intermediaries are allowed to do and what assets they can hold. Before you put your funds into a bank or some other such institution, you would want to know that your funds are safe and that the bank or other financial intermediary will be able to meet its obligations to you. One way of doing this is to restrict the financial intermediary from engaging in certain risky activities. For example some countries legislation separates commercial banking from the securities industry so that banks could not engage in risky ventures associated with this industry. Another way is to restrict financial intermediaries from holding certain risky assets, or at least from holding a greater quantity of these risky assets than is prudent. For example, commercial banks and other depository institutions are not allowed to hold common stock because stock prices experience substantial fluctuations. However, Insurance companies are allowed to hold common stock, but their holdings cannot exceed a certain fraction of their total assets.

d. **Financial activity regulation:**-These are rules about traders of securities and trading on financial markets. Probably the best example of this type of regulation is rules prohibiting the trading of a security by those who, because of their privileged position in a corporation, know more about the issuer's economic prospects than the general investing public. Such individuals are referred to as *insiders* and include, yet are not limited to, corporate managers and members of the board of directors. Trading by insiders (referred to as *insider trading*) is another problem posed by asymmetric information.

e. **Deposit Insurance:**-The government can insure people's deposits so that they do not suffer any financial loss if the financial intermediary that holds these deposits fails. All commercial and mutual savings banks, with a few minor exceptions, are required to enter deposit insurance, which is used to pay off depositors in the case of a bank's failure.

f. **Limits on Competition:** - Politicians have often declared that unbridled (uncontrolled) competition among financial intermediaries promotes failures that will harm the public. Although the evidence that competition does this is extremely weak, it has not stopped the state and federal governments from imposing many restrictive regulations.

g. **Restrictions on Interest Rates:**- Competition has also been inhibited by regulations that impose restrictions on interest rates that can be paid on deposits and loans.

4. *Arguments Regarding Regulation*

The financial system and institutions are among the most heavily regulated sectors of most economies. The government regulates financial markets and institutions for different reasons. But, there are different views as to the need and extent of Government intervention in financial markets. Arguments *in favourof* or *against* over regulations that are comments or opinions expressed on financial regulations by the *financial analysts, industry experts* and *economists etc.* are described as follow:-

1. **Arguments in favour of Regulations**

i.   **Ensures safety of the public funds**: - Elaborate government rules controlling what financial institutions can and cannot do arise from multiple causes. One is a concern about the safety of the public funds, especially the safety of the *savings* owned by millions of individuals and families. The reckless management and ultimate loss of personal savings can have devastating consequences for a family's future economic well-being and lifestyle, particularly at retirement. While savers have a responsibility to carefully evaluate the quality and stability of a financial institution before committing their savings to it, governments have long expressed a special concern for small savers who may lack the financial expertise and access to quality information necessary to be able to judge the true condition of a financial institution correctly. Moreover, many of the reasons that cause financial institutions to fail such as fraud, embezzlement, deteriorating loans, or manipulation of the books by insiders are often concealed from the public. Related to the desire for safety is a government's goal of promoting public confidence in the financial system. Unless the public is confident enough in the safety and security of their funds placed under the management of financial institutions, they will withdraw their savings and thereby reduce the volume of funds available for productive investment to construct new buildings, purchase new equipment, set up new businesses, and create new jobs. The economy's growth will slow and, over time, the public's standard of living will fall.

ii. **Help in the development of disadvantaged sectors**: - Regulations are often justified as the most direct way to aid so called "disadvantaged sectors" in the economy. Examples include farmers, small traders, new home buyers, and low-income families. Governments often place high social value and give importance for up-lifting these groups by guaranteeing loans made if possible with lower interest rates. If regulations are not there, this may not be possible for the governments. Governments also check the regional imbalance with regulations.

iii. **Help to check inflation**: - Financial institutions have the ability of creating money in the form credit cards, checkable deposits, and other accounts that can be used to make payments for the purchase of goods and services. History has shown that the creation of money is closely associated with inflation. Thus, the regulation of money creation has become a key objective of government activity in the financial sector.

iv. **Help in supporting Governments for funds and services**: - Finally, the enforcement of regulations for financial institutions has arisen because of governments depend upon financial institutions for funds and important services. Governments borrow money and depend upon financial institutions to buy a substantial proportion of government IOUs. Financial institutions also aid governments in the collection of tax revenue. Thus, governments frequently regulate financial institutions simply to ensure that these important benefits will continue to be provided to them.

2.   Arguments against Regulations

i.   **Creates moral hazard**: - Regulations cause depositors as well as financial institutions especially banks to behave less cautiously on the belief that the central bank is there to protect them in case of financial deterioration.

ii. **Agency capture**:- Regulators are ex-practitioners who share the same value as practitioners, and hence may be biased towards banks and insurance companies rather than money savers.

iii. **Increases cost of financial services**:- Adherence to regulations increase the costs to financial institutions and these costs may be passed on to clients in the form of financial services costs.

iv. **Gives room for monopolies to emerge**:- Regulations may restrain the entry of new companies and financial institutions. If the entry of new firms is restrained, true competition may not prevail in the markets. This situation gives room for monopolies to emerge. Because of monopolistic situation in the markets, consumers may not get quality services in spite of high cost of service they are paying.

v. **Leads to market inefficiency**: - Regulations sometimes not only restrain competition but also prevents mergers and acquisitions. This allows inefficient firms to stay in the markets.

5. *Who are the financial regulators?*

The financial regulation agencies are also called as financial regulators. Generally every country has its own financial system and like thus has/have financial regulators. Financial regulation agencies or bodies or regulators differ from country to country. In some countries, governments directly engage in financial regulation activity whereas in other countries, governments may appoint one or more such regulation bodies. These financial bodies or regulators are responsible to frame Regulatory Framework for the working of 156 financial markets and institutions in that country. Whenever need arises to re-assess the regulatory framework, financial regulators re-assess and bring new regulations to protect the interests of financial markets and institutions and investors. Generally, financial regulators include:

a) Ministry of Finance of the central government

b) Federal Reserve Bank or central bank of the country

c) Securities Exchange Commission

d) Insurance Regulatory Authority

e) Banking Regulation Authority etc

Chapter Six: - An Overview of Ethiopian Financial System

Leaning Objectives

At the end of the chapter students/learners will be able to.

- *Understand the financial sector development*
- *Appreciate the financial sector development in Ethiopia*
- *Recognize Ethiopian commodity exchange markets and its operation*

Text Box: Leaning Objectives At the end of the chapter students/learners will be able to. ü Understand the financial sector development ü Appreciate the financial sector development in Ethiopia ü Recognize Ethiopian commodity exchange markets and its operation

1. *Financial Markets and Institutions in Ethiopia*

Financial system is the collection of financial markets, institutions, instrument, laws, regulations, and techniques through which bonds, stocks, and other securities are traded, interest rates are determined, and financial services are produced and delivered around the world.

In the formal financial sector of Ethiopia banks take the dominant position financing the economy, however not large in number as well as in kind there are also non bank financial institutions mainly insurance companies and microfinance institutions. The financial system is also known with non existence formal capital market where long term equity and debt securities are traded. The Treasury bill market is the main financial market in Ethiopia in which 28 and 98 days government treasury bills are offered for auction to the general public, however the participants are mostly existing commercial banks. There is also an interbank money market in which the existing commercial banks are taking part and a foreign exchange market also functional in Ethiopia. The commodity market in which few major agricultural products are formally traded is the new phenomenon of the Ethiopian financial system.

2. *Financial Sector Development in Ethiopia*

The financial sector in Ethiopia consists of formal, semiformal and informal institutions. The **formal** financial system is a regulated sector which comprises of financial institutions such as banks, insurance companies and microfinance institutions. The saving and credit cooperative are considered as **semi-formal** financial institutions, which are not regulated and supervised by National Bank of Ethiopia (NBE). The **informal** financial sector in the country consists of unregistered traditional institutions such as *Iqub* (Rotating Savings and Credit Associations) *Idir* (Death Benefit Association) and money lenders.

i. Formal Financial Sector

Banks, insurance companies and micro finance institutions are the major financial institutions operating in Ethiopia.

a. Banks

Banking in Ethiopia started in 1905, with the establishment of the Bank of Abyssinia that was owned by the Ethiopian government in partnership with the National Bank of Egypt then under British rule. But a well-structured banking system started to evolve starting in the 1940s-after the Italian departure. A government owned bank-the State Bank of Ethiopia-was established in 1942, and a number of foreign bank branches and a private bank were operating in competition with the government owned commercial bank until they were nationalized and merged into one government owned mono-bank in 1976. The competitive banking situation that started to flourish during the 1960s and 1974s was nipped in the bud by the command system that reign over the 1974-1991 periods. Following the change of government in 1991, and the subsequent measures taken to liberalize and reorient the economy towards a system of economy based on commercial considerations, the financial market was deregulated. A proclamation number 84/94 was issued out to effect the deregulation and liberalization of the financial sector, and a number of private banks and insurance companies were established following the proclamation. Directives issued in subsequent years further deepen the liberalization mainly including the gradual liberalizations of the interest rate, foreign exchange determination, and money market operation. By the end of 2020/21, the number of banks reached 19, including the newly opened interest free bank (ZamZam bank) which opened 833 new branches during the review financial year, thereby raising the total number of bank branches to 7,344 from 6,511 last year. About 34.5 percent of the bank branches were located in Addis Ababa. As a result, one bank branch serves about 14,000 people[1].

[2]

Although one can observe a strong growth and revival of the private sector since liberalization in the 1990s; yet, the state-owned banks seem to dominate the industry. Despite some improvement in the sector in the last couples of years, Ethiopian banking remains in its low status. For instance, the estimates of Bank's recent *Financial Sector Diagnostic* show that less than 10% of households have access to formal credit (African Development Bank, 2011). In general, the sector is characterized by small banking, limited range of services, absence of capital markets and the sector largely remains closed to foreign investors.

b. Insurance Company

Likewise to banking, Ethiopia's insurance industry is undeveloped. Its emergence is traced back to the establishment of the Bank of Abyssinia in 1905. The Bank had been acting as an agent for foreign insurance companies to underwrite fire and marine policies. Before liberalization the command economy including political instability had been the stumbling block for the growth of the financial sector in Ethiopia.

The 1990's ushered in economic liberalization that led to the revival of private sector participation in the financial sector. This has led to the formation of a number of private insurance companies. Similarly, the number of insurance companies stood at 18, whose branches rose to 632 after they opened 27 new branches in 2020/21. Of the total branches, about 54.6 percent of total insurance branches were situated in Addis Ababa. 85.8 percent were private insurance companies. Insurance companies increased their total capital by 14.7 percent to Birr 11.1 billion whose share of private insurance companies was 73.6 percent and that of public insurance company was 26.4 percent.

[3]

Accordingly the insurance market is undeveloped, uncompetitive and there exist paucity of information on the kind of life insurance that is currently present. The current practice of bulk of insurance coverage and business in Ethiopia is targeting the corporate market and focuses mainly on general insurance with a very limited coverage in life insurance. The insurance sector is dependent on the banking sector for much of its new business. Most Ethiopian insurance companies have sister banks and its common for these banks to refer their clients to their sister insurance companies, but this is largely restricted to credit life insurance products.

c. **Microfinance Institutions**

The emergence of Microfinance institution is a recent phenomenon in Ethiopia compared to other developing countries. The first microfinance service in Ethiopia was introduced as an experiment in 1994, when the Relief Society of Tigray (REST) attempted to rehabilitate drought and war affected people through the rural credit scheme. It was inspired by other countries' experiences and adapted to the conditions of the Tigray region (northern part of Ethiopia). In the second half of the 1990s, as a result of its success, the microfinance service was gradually replicated in other regions. The Ethiopian microfinance industry has undergone tremendous growth and development in a very short period of time. At the same time, the number of micro[1]finance institutions (MFIs) reached 39, whose total capital and total asset increased by 43.4 and 13.8 percent and stood at Birr 27.9 billion and Birr 105 billion, respectively. In addition, MFIs' deposit mobilization and credit expanded remarkably.

[4]

Similar to microfinance approaches in many other parts of the world, MFIs in Ethiopia focus on group-based lending and promote compulsory and voluntary savings. They use joint liability, social pressure, and compulsory savings as alternatives to conventional forms of collateral. These institutions provide financial service, mainly credit and saving and, in some cases, loan insurance. The objectives of MFIs are quite similar across organizations. Almost all MFIs in the country have poverty alleviation as an objective. They focus on reducing poverty and vulnerability of poor households by increasing agricultural productivity and incomes, diversifying off farm sources of income, and building household assets. They seek to achieve these objectives by expanding access to financial services through large and sustainable microfinance institutions.

ii. Semiformal Financial Sector

Savings and credit cooperatives are type of organizations providing financial services to the poor in rural areas of Ethiopia. These include multi-purpose and credit and saving cooperatives.

v. Saving and Credit Cooperatives

The history of formal or Modern types of cooperative development in Ethiopia started in the Era of Emperor Haile Selassie I between 1950 and 1974. The predominant societies were producers and service co-operatives. Since this time cooperative policy and law has undertaken many reforms and cooperatives have come to play a crucial role in economic and social development. To facilitate the establishment of modern cooperatives, Cooperative Decree 44/1961 and Proclamation 241/1966 were issued.

Aided by the Cooperative Societies Proclamation No. 147/1991, cooperatives started to see changes for better opportunities as their roles in economic development were objectively understood. By Cooperative Proclamation No. 147/1998, the legality of cooperatives had been acknowledged by Federal Democratic Republic of Ethiopia's (FDRE) Constitution which is the supreme law of the land. Currently the law governing Cooperative in Ethiopia is new Cooperative Proclamation No.985/2016 that came to existence on Dec. 2016 after repealing the previous Cooperative Proclamation No 147/1991. Cooperatives in Ethiopia are playing an active role in the fields of finance, input and output marketing, consumer goods, agro processing, mechanization and many other social and economic activities. In Ethiopia there are three types of saving and credit cooperatives, namely Institution based SACCOs; Community based SACCOS; and SACCOs sponsored by NGOs. Unlike other formal financial institutions (banks and micro finance institutions), saving and credit cooperatives are owned, controlled and capitalized by their members. This implies that the savings and credit cooperatives are not subjected to supervision and regulation of the National Bank of Ethiopia. The ministry of cooperatives is responsible for the coordination of their activities. One of the principles of SACCOs is that lending is limited to only members of the cooperatives and the amount of loan depends on the level of individual saving deposits. One of the weaknesses reflected in the co-operative sector is poor administrative and financial management. On the other hand the government through the relevant ministry is not adequately equipped to monitor and control the cooperative movement. Savings and credit cooperatives in Ethiopia are not permitted to take deposits from nonmembers.

Many rural saving and credit cooperatives provide loan services for agricultural inputs, animal fattening and in some cases for off farm activities. Loan disbursement policies are prudent, only those with sufficient savings and collateral can lend. The majority of loans are provided for a period of one year or less. Usually interest on loans is higher than charged by commercial banks but often lower than that of MFI's and definitely lower than the money lenders rate.

Cooperatives have played a significant role towards achieving the growth and poverty reduction strategy by promoting income generating activities and improving access to near banking services to rural and urban households. According to Federal Cooperative Agency (FCA) official report (2021)1, there are more than 92755 cooperatives in Ethiopia with 21,043,370 members (6,743,429 female and 14,299,941 male) and there are **21,328 primary SACCOS** and they have 5,384,559 members (3,122,454 female and 2,262,105 male)[5].

iii. Informal Financial Sector

In both rural and urban areas in Ethiopia, it is common that neighboring family households organize themselves and develop their own institutions, popularly known as Community-Based Organizations (CBOs). The nature of the CBOs highly varies from social, religious and financial concerns, but are all aimed to address the needs of the people. In most communities, membership in traditional community associations such as *iddirs, iqqubs* and *mehabers* are very common. More importantly, these traditional institutions also play a crucial role in savings and beneficiary mobilization in the informal financial sector.

a. *Iddirs*

An *Iddir* is the most common informal institution in Ethiopia, common in both rural and urban areas. It is an association made up by a group of persons united by ties of family and friendship, by living in the same district, by jobs, or by belonging to the same ethnic group and as an object of providing mutual aid and financial assistance in certain circumstances. It is primarily a burial society whereby savings are made to cover the cost of funerals, but also weddings. Whenever a death occurs among its members, the organization raises an amount of money to handle the burial and other related ceremonies. It further aims to address different community concerns and provides various services to its members. Membership is regularly by residence, whereby members pay a small monthly fee.

During the current rule of the Ethiopia People's Revolutionary Democratic Front (EPRDF), the potential of *iddirs* as a vehicle for development has been further acknowledged by both the government as well as by nongovernmental institutions (NGOs). From the government's point of view, the general recognition of civil society's role in development has led to that *iddirs* have been accepted as possible partners for successful and sustainable development.

b. *Iqqubs*

Iqqubs have played a significant role especially for the informal sector in Ethiopia. An *iqqub* is a traditional saving and credit association (Rotating Saving and Credit association), of which its purpose is basically to pool the savings of their members in accordance with the rules established by the group. Members usually deposit contributions on a weekly or monthly basis, and lots are drawn by turns so that the one who wins the chance gets the total sum. This process continues on a regular basis until the last member receives his/ her share or what she/he has been saving through the months and the whole process starts again.

c. *Mehabers*

Another common CBO is the *Mehaber*, which is a religious, informal institution that aims to raise funds for medical and burial expenses. It is widespread among the Orthodox Christians of Ethiopia, as it typically draws its members from the church. Members usually meet on a monthly basis for food and drink, and commonly support each other in times of difficulty.

3. *Regulation of Financial Sector in Ethiopia*

Major economic reforms have been taken by the Ethiopian government after the fall of the socialist government in 1991. Consequently, the Ethiopian Financial System has passed through significant reform process since 1992 as a part of transition from a planned to a market economy. Prior to this reform process, there had not been any competition within the financial sector due to the fact that all of the formal financial institutions were state owned and private financial institutions were not allowed to operate.

After the implementation of the reform process starting from 1992, there have been significant measures undertaken by the government. The major reform measures taken include: Liberalizing and reforming the financial sector, relaxing foreign exchange controls, dismantling the administered interest rate regime, establishing a new regulatory framework for banks, insurance companies, microfinance institutions and cooperatives. The Ethiopian Financial system, generally speaking falls into three categories. These include: Formal, semi-formal and informal financial system. The formal financial system is a regulated sector, which is well organized and provides financial services mainly to urban areas.

The following describes the minimum capital requirement for banking, insurance and microfinance business in Ethiopia[6].

- *Minimum capital requirement for **banks** Directive N̲o̲: - **SBB/78/2021** state that he minimum paid-up capital required to obtain a banking business license shall be **Birr 5 Billion (Five Billion Birr)**, which shall be fully paid in cash and deposited in a bank (s) in the name and to the account of the bank under formation.*
- *Minimum paid up capital for **insurance company** Directive N̲o̲: - **SIB/57/2022** general insurance license requires Birr **400 Million**, long term insurance business **100 Million**. The minimum paid up capital required to obtain both general and long term insurance business license shall be birr **500 million** which ought to be fully paid up in cash and deposited in blocked account in the name of the insurance company to be established.*
- *Minimum Capital Requirement for **microfinance** Directives No. **MFI/ 25 /2013** The minimum initial paid up capital required to obtain a micro- financing business license shall be **Birr 2,000,000 (Birr two million)**, which*

shall be fully paid in cash and deposited in a bank in the name and to the account of the microfinance institution under formation.

In the wake of the global financial crisis, many developed and developing country governments are prioritizing stability at the individual financial institutions and systemic level by strengthening financial regulation. Even though the latter is important to make financial systems more robust, its contribution to inclusive growth might be insufficient, especially in poor countries.

4. *Ethiopian Commodity Exchange Market and Its Operation*

Commodity trading has existed for hundreds of years. The first commodity exchanges were in Asia where Japan established an exchange for rice in Osaka in the 17th century and traded with futures contracts as early as 1697, almost two centuries before they were used in the United States in 1867.

ECX's establishment is founded on Proclamation No. 550/2007. This proclamation mandates ECX to develop its own rules for the governance of its various operations. Further, the Ethiopia Commodity Exchange Authority (ECEA) a regulatory body of the ECX was established by Proclamation 551/2007.

The Rules of the Exchange developed by ECX provide the blueprint for all rules governing membership, management, trading, warehousing, clearing and settlement, and other operations of ECX, in addition to the conduct of its members. ECX maintains a careful approach to monitoring and tracking the adequacy and performance of its members, as well as their behavior vis-à-vis their clients in the market. In line with global best practices, ECX experts regularly conduct surveillance on market trends as well as conducting audit and investigations on market operations to protect the market from manipulation, excessive speculation, fraud, or other malpractice.

Ethiopia Commodity Exchange, or ECX, launched in 2008 with the goal of transforming the country's agricultural sector. ECX creates opportunities for unparalleled growth in the commodity sector and linked industries, such as transport and logistics, banking and financial services, and others.

The Ethiopia Commodity Exchange (ECX), as it is officially known, will provide a marketplace where buyers and sellers can come together to trade and be assured of quality, delivery and payment. The exchange includes a trading floor in Addis Ababa, six warehouse delivery locations, and 20 electronic price tickers in major market towns

The Ethiopia Commodity Exchange (ECX) is a national multi-commodity exchange in Ethiopia that brings together buyers and sellers of agricultural commodities. Participants on the ECX trade spot contracts that standardize the *quality*, *quantity*, *payment*, and *delivery* of agricultural goods.
A **spot price** is the price to settle a commodity contract *immediately*. The participants settle "on the spot." A *futures* contract is settled in the future, *not immediately*.

What Can You Trade at ECX?

ECX offers customers access to trading and/or clearing for a variety of agricultural products.
Description: C:\Users\user\Desktop\ECX.jpg

How is ECX Regulated?

The proclamation that established the ECX mandates the exchange to set out its own rules for self-governance of its various operations. At the same time, a second proclamation established an outside regulatory body for the ECX – the Ethiopia Commodity Exchange Authority (ECEA).

Self-Governing Rules

The rules of the exchange developed by ECX list the regulations governing membership, management, trading, warehousing, clearing and settlement, and other operations of ECX. The rules also cover the conduct of its members.

Ethiopia Commodity Exchange Authority Rules

The ECEA has the authority to oversee the following:-

- Exchange members and their representatives
- Clearing institutions (domestic banks or other financial institutions engaged in clearing and settlement of payments)
- Rules of the exchange and regulation of exchange-traded contracts
- The conduct of investment advisors, consulting companies, law practices, accounting and audit professionals, as this conduct pertains to ECX business.

ECEA also has the authority to investigate wrongdoing and adjudicate complaints falling under its jurisdiction. ECEA can, when appropriate, refer criminal cases to the appropriate court. As part of its oversight, ECEA issues directives regarding its activities.

How Does the ECX Conduct Trading? The ECX is a spot exchange, which means the participants settle prices and delivery "on the spot," or immediately. Traders and their representatives trade more than 200 spot contracts on the ECX.

Where Do Contracts Trade?

The ECX has an octagonal trading pit where trading takes place via "open outcry". In this method of trading, a trader announces his/her intention to buy (bid) or sell (offer) a particular contract, the quantity he/she wants to buy, and the price he/she is willing to pay. Other market participants can make a counter bid or offer or accept the terms offered by the trader.

How Do Traders Communicate?

Traders on the ECX use hand signals to convey their intentions. A trader first announces the commodity and then the quantity. If the trader wishes to buy the commodity, the trader turns the palm of his/her hand toward his/her face. If the trader wishes to sell the commodity, the trader turns his/her palm away from the face.

Clearing and Settlement

ECX's zero default, fast and efficient Clearing and Settlement department assumes Central Counter Party (CCP) risk for all members trades. It establishes the net obligations of each member, informs the members of their daily net obligations and transfers cash funds and commodity ownership among members. Commodity ownership is primarily transferred by Central Depository of the Exchange while conducting title transfer for cash and commodity every next day after trade.

The Settlement Transactions

Balance Enquiry on Pay-in accounts
10:00AM on the day of trading (for afternoon Trading)
04:00PM on day before Trading (T-1)
Member Pay-In (to ECX)
08:00–09:00 next working day (T+1)
Member Pay-Out (from ECX)

11:00-12:00 next working day (T+1)

Banks and Branches:-Currently ECX is working with sixteen settlement banks. These banks have dedicated ECX settlement team in their Head Office:

F. Commercial Bank of Ethiopia (CBE)
F. Dashen Bank S.C
F. Awash International Bank S.C
F. United Bank S.C
F. NIB International Bank S.C.
F. Wegagen Bank S.C.
F. Bank of Abyssinia S.C.
F. Oromia International Bank S.C.
F. Lion International Bank S.C.
F. Construction & Business Bank S.C.
F. Cooperative Bank of Oromia S.C.
F. Buna international bank
F. Birhan international bank
F. Abay Bank
F. ENAT Bank

All ECX accounts MUST be in a networked branch.[7]

References:-

1. Cecchetti, Stephen G. and Schoenholtz, Kermit L., (2017). **Money, Banking, and Financial Markets** 5th ed. McGraw-Hill Education, USA.
2. Frank J. Fabozzi, Franco Modigfiani, Frank J. Jones, (2010). **Foundations of Financial Markets and Institutions** 4th ed. Pearson Education, Inc, USA.
3. Frederic S. Mishkin and Stanley G. Eakins,(2012). **Financial Markets and Institutions** 7th ed. Pearson Education Limited, USA.
4. Frederic S. Mishkin and Stanley G. Eakins,(2018). **Financial Markets and Institutions** 9th global ed. Pearson Education Limited, UK.
5. Mishkin F., Matthews K and Giuliodori M.(2013). **The Economics of Money, Banking and Financial Markets** European ed. Pearson Education Limited, UK.
6. Bliss, R.R. and Kaufman, G.G. (Ed). (2008). **Financial Institutions and Markets**: Current Issues in Financial Markets. 1st ed. USA, Palgrave Macmillan.
7. Saunders, Anthony, Marcia Millon Cornett, (2015). **Financial Markets and Institutions** 6th ed. McGraw-Hill Education, USA.
8. Proclamation N<u>o</u>:-1159/2019. **Proclamation for Banking Business**. Addis Ababa, Ethiopia.
9. Proclamation No:-1163/2019. **Proclamation for Insurance Business**. Addis Ababa, Ethiopia.
10. Proclamation No:-1164/2019. **Proclamation for Microfinance Business**. Addis Ababa, Ethiopia.
11. Proclamation No:-591/2008. **Proclamation for the National Bank of Ethiopia Establishment**. Addis Ababa, Ethiopia.
12. Regulations and Directives related to financial institution in Ethiopia.

--//----------------------------------

[1] NBE Annual report 2020/21: PP 39

[2] NBE Annual report 2020/21: PP 40

[3] NBE Annual report 2020/21: PP 41

[4] NBE Annual report 2020/21: PP 42

[5] FCA report 2021

[6]www.nbe.gov.et /directives

[7]www.ecx.com.et

Contents

CPSIA information can be obtained
at www.ICGtesting.com
Printed in the USA
BVHW021426280623
666442BV00013B/473